# Theorizing in Comparative Politics

This book addresses a pertinent issue in comparative politics: how can the discipline do analytical justice to regions of the world that differ historically from the Western experience? For decades the West has served as a baseline against which all other regions are assessed, most recently in studies of democratization. Structural differences between regions have been ignored in favour of explanations based on human agency and institutions. In *Theorizing in Comparative Politics*, Goran Hyden uses the countries of Africa as an empirical case to demonstrate what a structural approach adds to the comparative study of democracy. Priorities such as state-building challenge the effort to shape democratic regimes and call for explanations that recognize the impact of local power dynamics on the prospects for democratic development. Informative and thoughtful, this book sheds light on issues that have been underexplored in the field in recent years.

GORAN HYDEN is a distinguished professor emeritus in the Department of Political Science at the University of Florida. *Theorizing in Comparative Politics* is the result of sixty years of research and teaching shared between East Africa and Florida. Earlier iterations of the work include *Political Development in Rural Tanzania* (1969), *No Shortcuts to Progress* (1983), and *African Politics in Comparative Perspective* (2006).

# Theorizing in Comparative Politics

## Democratization in Africa

GORAN HYDEN
*University of Florida*

CAMBRIDGE UNIVERSITY PRESS

Shaftesbury Road, Cambridge CB2 8EA, United Kingdom

One Liberty Plaza, 20th Floor, New York, NY 10006, USA

477 Williamstown Road, Port Melbourne, VIC 3207, Australia

314–321, 3rd Floor, Plot 3, Splendor Forum, Jasola District Centre,
New Delhi – 110025, India

103 Penang Road, #05–06/07, Visioncrest Commercial, Singapore 238467

Cambridge University Press is part of Cambridge University Press & Assessment,
a department of the University of Cambridge.

We share the University's mission to contribute to society through the pursuit of
education, learning and research at the highest international levels of excellence.

www.cambridge.org
Information on this title: www.cambridge.org/9781009429511

DOI: 10.1017/9781009429528

First published 2024

*A catalogue record for this publication is available from the British Library*

*Library of Congress Cataloging-in-Publication Data*
Names: Hydén, Göran, 1938– author.
Title: Theorizing in comparative politics : democratization in Africa /
Göran Hydén.
Description: Cambridge, United Kingdom ; New York, NY : Cambridge
University Press, 2024. | Includes bibliographical references and index.
Identifiers: LCCN 2023025728 | ISBN 9781009429511 (hardback) |
ISBN 9781009429528 (ebook)
Subjects: LCSH: Democratization – Africa. | Political culture – Africa. |
Postcolonialism – Africa. | Africa – Politics and government – 1945–1960. |
Africa – Politics and government – 1960–
Classification: LCC JQ1879.A15 H94 2024 | DDC 320.46–dc23/eng/20230824
LC record available at https://lccn.loc.gov/2023025728

ISBN 978-1-009-42951-1 Hardback
ISBN 978-1-009-42949-8 Paperback

# Contents

v

# Figures

# Tables

# Introduction

The purpose of this book is to examine theorizing in Comparative Politics using Africa as empirical reference to highlight the problems of mainstreaming regions outside the West into studies of democratization. It tries to demonstrate how countries that do not resemble the model of already developed and democratic societies become mere add-ons in comparisons claiming universal validity. Comparativists, especially in the West, treat democracy as the world's default position. In most countries elsewhere in the world, however, politics is not infused with democratic values. Yet, for decades now, little attention has been paid to these alternative modes of conducting politics. They have been analysed in a rather perfunctory way using a democracy lens. The general tendency to refer to these countries as "hybrid" or "autocratic" is an example of the level of imperiousness that sometimes manifests itself in the field. Such self-assurance, however, easily backfires. Reality soon catches up with its assumptions, as the cases of democratic backsliding and the rise of autocratic regimes indicate. With the ongoing changes in the structural and demographic context of the world, the time has come to identify their implications for the study of Comparative Politics.

As someone who started his career as comparativist over sixty years ago I have been along and active in the discipline ever since the birth of our field as we know it today. My inspiration was the seminal book edited by Gabriel Almond and James Coleman titled *The Politics of the Developing Areas*, published in 1960. Its significance might be hard to fully appreciate today but no publication has in my view played a greater role in the evolution of Comparative Politics.

It helped establish the field as a prominent part of political science. It also brought developing areas, and especially Africa, into prominence in a blossoming field of Comparative Politics fuelled by large amounts of US federal money during the Kennedy administration in support of area studies research. It was in this virtually celebratory atmosphere in the discipline that I chose Africa as the focus of my own Comparative Politics research.

I have lived and worked in East Africa for a third of my life. I have done research and been teaching the first generation of political science students at Makerere University in Uganda, University of Nairobi in Kenya, and University of Dar es Salaam in Tanzania. This experience has shaped my own outlook on the discipline. Africa to me is not just "a piece of real estate" to be assessed but a meaningful point of reference in both my everyday life and academic work. When it comes to the study of African politics, I am not merely an outsider looking in.

Area-oriented studies provide the necessary empirical input for comparison. In the early 1960s there was little published about the new states that had become political systems of their own after the Second World War. In these circumstances it is no surprise that the early attempts at comparison were heavy on theory and light on facts. This ambition to accurately reflect political reality while also developing theory for cross-national comparison has continued to constitute the energy that drives the field forward. There may be little agreement regarding how this balancing act should be carried out. After all, Comparative Politics is not paradigmatic in ways that allow for the pursuit of what Kuhn (1962) has labelled "normal science", that is, the conduct of research within a single theoretical frame over an extended time. Attempts have been made in this direction, but they have faltered, and the field has reverted to recognizing complexity and thus the scope for multiple lines of inquiry. This suggests that the mode by which Comparative Politics advances is dialectical rather than linear. We do not build knowledge into a single tower. Our effort instead produces less impressive pillars of knowledge in tension with one another. In comparing our scientific ambition to that of researchers in the physical or natural sciences we have reason to be humble. The political system is not a piece of rock. Nor is it, like the human body, a virtually closed system.

In hindsight, it is possible to identify three main attempts at consolidating the study of Comparative Politics under a single over-arching theory. The *first* was the use of structural functionalism in the early 1960s, which argued that all political systems share the same functions but differ in their degree of structural differentia-tion. The purpose of this approach was to move beyond an old form of institutionalism focused on the study of constitutions to inte-grate the analysis of all political systems into a single meta-theory. Its momentum, however, stalled quite quickly because the theory proved too abstract for meaningful empirical application. It was also widely criticized by neo-Marxist scholars for taking for granted that development – or modernization – is a linear process with win-win outcomes (e.g., Rodney 1972; Amin 1976). Instead, they launched their own underdevelopment theory based on the assumption that development is a zero-sum game with strong nations being winners and weak ones, losers.

The *second* attempt twenty years later was the rise of rational choice theory to argue that political actors regardless of culture aim at maximizing their own utility (Bates 1981; Ostrom 1990). Its pur-pose was to standardize the premises on which to analyse political behaviour and choice. It suffered a similar fate although primarily because of its arrogance – the notion that only self-interest counts. Its position was challenged by the rise of constructivism – the idea that knowledge is not absolute but subject to change depending on circumstances (Hay 2002). This implies not only that knowledge is created through interaction with others but also that it can be deconstructed and replaced by alternative formulas for understand-ing reality. This politicization of formal knowledge has become

Table I.1 *Summary of theories used for mainstreaming Comparative Politics*

| Category | Structural functionalism | Rational choice theory | Democratic theory |
|---|---|---|---|
| Underlying assumption | All systems are the same | Maximization of own utility | Own normativity |
| Objective | Integrationist | Standardizing | Evaluative |
| Shortcoming | Too abstract | Too arrogant | Reductionist |
| Critique | Underdevelopment theory | Constructivism | Contextualism |

*Source:* Author

a prominent feature of political analysis and spread into political practice, as evident for instance in accusations that facts are "fake".

The *third* try has been the more recent use of democratic theory to study political systems. Its focus has been on voluntary and institutional choices at the expense of structural legacies. The purpose of applying this theory has been to lay the ground for evaluating where countries rank on a global scale of democracy. As democratization has slowed down – and in some places been replaced by its opposite, autocratization (Luhrmann and Lindberg 2019) – scholarly interest has shifted to examining the conditions in which democracy may develop and flourish (Möller and Skaaning 2018). Democracy is not the only game in town. Furthermore, it is being played differently depending on a series of factors that have largely been ignored in the dominant literature on democratization that strives to measure its success. The analysis of democracy in Comparative Politics, therefore, needs to be turned around: make it the key variable to be explained. Its value as an explanatory variable in the field is history.

The aforementioned three theoretical attempts at consolidation (summarized in Table I.1) have one significant thing in common: they are all developed on the premise that West European society provides the model to copy. They take for granted that other countries in the world are ready to embrace this model and have the capacity to implement it. The limits of this ethnocentric preconception are the subject of the chapters that follow in this volume.

In each instance when the leading theory begins to lose its relevance and appeal, it has been followed by a spouting of alternative explanations. Today this rise of new approaches emerges in the wake of democratic theory's inability to offer persuasive-enough explanations. A historical and thicker approach to explaining the variations between regions and countries is viewed here as filling the voids left behind by the almost exclusive focus on measures of success in realizing democratic values. It entails shifting the balance in favour of a more open-ended approach that helps explain the underlying conditions of political development today. This is as relevant in countries that suffer democratic backsliding as it is in countries like those in Africa where the challenge continues to be that of filling the democratic glass half full. Area knowledge becomes more precious in these attempts to answer the questions of not only when and where but also how and why. Regions follow different cycles of governance, and the narrative produced by democratic theory in Europe or Latin America does not necessarily fit everywhere. The research challenge is to find out why that is the case. In examining the content of three main journals in the field, *Comparative Politics*, *Comparative Political Studies*, and *Studies in Comparative International Development*, it is evident (see Table I.2) that in trying to answer the "why" question greater attention to Africa and the Middle East is warranted. They belong to the least covered regions. The fact that a definite number of studies on African politics get published in some of the many multidisciplinary journals devoted to the African region, notably *African Affairs*, *Journal of Modern African Studies*, *Africa Spectrum* (published in Hamburg), and *African Studies Review*, does not reduce the region's marginal status in Comparative Politics theorizing.

In making his comparison with International Relations, Caporaso (2000) suggested that the main feature of Comparative Politics is the tension between the generality of theory and the explanatory accuracy that makes concession to time and place.

Table I.2 *Distribution of general and area-oriented articles in Comparative Politics journals at three intervals**

| Category | General | Latin America | Europe | Post-Soviet | Asia | Africa | Middle East | Australia Pacific |
|---|---|---|---|---|---|---|---|---|
| *Comparative Politics* | | | | | | | | |
| 2019–21 | 15 | 17 | 5 | 15 | 12 | 10 | 7 | 0 |
| 2009–11 | 15 | 15 | 9 | 11 | 13 | 4 | 2 | 0 |
| 1999–2001 | 14 | 12 | 9 | 6 | 8 | 8 | 0 | 0 |
| *Comparative Political Studies* | | | | | | | | |
| 2019–21 | 148 | 22 | 23 | 7 | 26 | 18 | 2 | 0 |
| 2009–11 | 79 | 15 | 30 | 14 | 6 | 7 | 5 | 1 |
| 1999–2001 | 57 | 12 | 23 | 3 | 7 | 3 | 1 | 0 |
| *Studies in Comparative International Development* | | | | | | | | |
| 2019–21 | 30 | 8 | 2 | 0 | 19 | 8 | 0 | 0 |
| 2009–11 | 18 | 14 | 0 | 0 | 2 | 3 | 7 | 0 |
| 1999–2001 | 18 | 31 | 0 | 0 | 3 | 3 | 1 | 0 |
| Total | 394 | 146 | 101 | 56 | 96 | 64 | 25 | 1 |

* Articles that are comparing multiple countries or are genuinely cross-national are coded as "general" together with those that address an overarching issue, for example, theory or method. The rest are coded by area, where "post-Soviet" includes the countries in Eastern Europe and Central Asia.

*Source:* Author

Unlike International Relations theorists, who focus on the distribution of power and strategic interaction in an environment guided by law and morality, dominant comparativist theorizing starts from the premise that political systems are already organized hierarchies of authority. The focus of research, therefore, becomes institutions.

The lack of attention to power is evident in liberal political economy studies. They start from the assumption that societies are organized around economic interests that compete with one another in an institutional equilibrium (e.g., Weingast and Wittman 2006; Haggard and Kaufman 2016). The distribution of goods or services may not be equal but the costs of "rocking the boat" are deemed by any party to be too high. Actors, therefore, are ready to accept suboptimal outcomes to keep the system going. Such is the principal characterization of the political economy of developed societies. It is much less applicable to Africa where the main threat to political stability stems from the struggle to align political regimes to the challenges of state-building. Political actors are foremost preoccupied with the distribution of power to be able to institutionalize a political order of their liking. Valuable accounts of these power relations and the regime breakdown that they may cause include Botchwey (1981), Anyang Nyong'o (1987), and Himmelstrand et al. (1994).

This book recognizes that Comparative Politics theorizing in the last few decades has generated interesting insights into how democracy is at play in countries around the world. This dominant orientation in the research community, however, has not given sufficient attention to what it means for a country to be "developing" or "democratizing". The institutional challenges are quite different between countries that are already developed and democratic, on the one hand, and those that battle to get there, on the other. In regions like Africa politics is understandably about institutionalizing not just the process of policy making but also the framework that determines the nature of political conduct. Democracy is not a given but a good that political actors seek in competition with other values and priorities. This calls for a different way of theorizing – one that treats democracy as a dependent variable in its broader social and economic context.

One reason why the study of democratization in Africa has been so extensively driven by reference to the Western experience is the shortage of input by African scholars to the mainstream of the field. Many have made valuable contributions through theoretically informed monographs focused on a single country. Others like Chege (1995), Ake (1996), Adejumobi (2015), and Durotoye (2017) have attempted broader overviews of democracy in Africa that have left marks but not changed the Comparative Politics mainstream. This book builds on the contributions by these African and non-African scholars.

It begins with a discussion in Chapter 1 of the three theoretical spurts that have occurred in Comparative Politics since the 1960s, focusing on the implications for the study of African politics. Chapter 2 traces the historical roots of African development going back to pre-colonial times when the region was confined to the margins of development taking place in other regions and showing how this legacy is alive even today. Chapter 3 turns to the colonial period and how foreign powers shaped a social dynamic that is different from the "core" regions of Europe and the Americas. Chapter 4 builds on the previous two to discuss the issues of forging a durable political community. It focuses on the special nature of Africa's state-nations in comparison with the standard nation-state concept drawn from the historical experience elsewhere. Successfully constructing the nation is dependent on rules and norms that give the process its legitimacy. Chapter 5 discusses how regimes are cobbled together in response to the post-colonial challenges African leaders encounter in stabilizing their political community. Chapter 6 focuses on the role of political parties in mobilizing followers and contributing to policymaking. It highlights the transactional nature of party politics in the region and the limited role that ideology plays as guide to policy. Chapter 7 examines the issue of building trust in a cultural context where identity tends to be a stronger driving force than economic interests organized into social classes. Chapter 8 is a comparative study of four countries in East Africa that share a similar colonial experience yet have developed different regimes to tackle their post-colonial challenges. Chapter 9, the final chapter, aims at pulling together the findings in previous chapters, identifying the new challenges for comparative political analysis, and discussing how politics might be approached in a way that brings Africa back to the centre stage of Comparative Politics theorizing.

# I  Three Theoretical Spurts

## I.I  INTRODUCTION

Theory is what guides research. Without it, there would be no organized knowledge to divide into disciplines, fields, or sub-fields. Theory is built on symbolic representations called concepts or, usually, constructs when referring to something abstract, like regime or state. It becomes the lens through which we acquire knowledge about such key variables as political behaviour, choice, and performance. Theory in the social sciences, however, is not written in stone and undergoes change as it is continuously being tested in new research. This allows us to appreciate the dynamic but also volatile nature of our subject matter, politics. It reminds us of the challenges that exist in our ambition to enhance the growth of a body of accepted scientific knowledge. Political science is not like the physical sciences where researchers can hang on to one and the same theory, or paradigm, until something earth-shaking occurs. This gives physicists plenty of time to solve puzzles within a single and common theoretical frame. They can enjoy long periods of "normal science". Questioning the dominant theory in the hard sciences is risky and associated with possible ostracism. (Those who take the risk, however, stand the biggest chance of earning a Nobel Prize!)

Social scientists share the ambition of accumulating knowledge through the use of scientific theory, but because politics is unpredictable, stabilizing the generation of knowledge by hanging on to a single theory has its limits. Anomalies that challenge a dominant theory are many (Geddes 2010). Periods of pursuing normal science, therefore, tend to become short. Alternative theories lie waiting around the corner. This tension between constancy and renewal has been and still is a prominent feature of Comparative Politics. It becomes especially evident in an Africanist perspective. Because generalizations are derived from theories meant to highlight what is an already "developed" or "democratic" society, Africa, still developing and democratizing, demonstrates features that make it different in comparison not only with Western Europe and North America but also with other regions such as Latin America and Eastern Europe. The political issue in Africa is not the backsliding experience of countries with a democratic tradition. Instead, it is how to build democracy in a context where its benefits were denied to the local population by the colonial administrators. This chapter is devoted to highlighting how social scientists have built theoretical constructs with the aim of strengthening the comparative analysis of politics.

## I.2   THREE THEORETICAL BREAKTHROUGHS

The literature on African politics has been driven by two main concerns: (1) to find its place in the pantheon of mainstream theories and (2) to highlight its innate dynamics. The two do not come together easily: the first fosters a search for generalities, the second for empirical manifestations in local space. This tension is striking when examining how African politics has been approached in Comparative Politics since it was founded in the middle of the last century. This examination shows a back-and-forth movement between an emphasis on theoretical integration, on the one hand, and fresh empirical insights and alternative theoretical explanations, on the other. The former has driven the discipline's development while the latter has served as its corrective. Because politics is not inanimate, theory in the social sciences invites constant reassessment. This chapter will render the story of how the study of African politics has fared in this process.

As indicated in the Introduction, it is possible to identify three theoretical spurts in Comparative Politics that have shaped its evolution: (1) structural functionalism in the 1960s, (2) rational choice theory in the 1980s, and (3) democratic theory in the 2000s. Each one has been an attempt to redefine the field in response to changes in global politics. Each of these spurts has had a major impact on the study of African politics. It is necessary, therefore, to begin with an account of these dominant theories and their particulars.

To begin, this table summary tells us quite a bit about Comparative Politics as a field of study in political science. First, for its own advancement it has gathered inspiration from neighbouring disciplines. Theories developed by anthropologists and sociologists helped transform political science in the 1960s when it abandoned an outdated institutionalism wedded to the study of laws and constitutions. Second, while there has been a continuous ambition to find a general or grand theory to explain political phenomena, the more striking impression is how widely the search for universality has been, covering structural as well as institutional and agency-based explanations. Third, it is not difficult to see that the high ambitions generated by each spurt have caused their own response in the form of critique and reconceptualization of the subject matter. The rest of this chapter will address these issues by elaborating on the contents of Table 1.1.

### 1.2.1  Structural Functionalism

The first generation of comparativists was especially ambitious in their attempt to develop a theory that could explain politics regardless of context. The structural-functionalist approach – which was developed in the late 1950s by a team of sociologists and political scientists, many with knowledge of different regions of the world, and articulated in an edited volume on the politics in developing areas (Almond and Coleman 1960) – treated the political system as an organism in which all parts were connected through their own feedback loops. Their challenge was how to conduct inquiries about societies for which a previously accumulated literature was lacking (Almond 1960). A good deal of attention was devoted to the elaboration of conceptual schemes that could lead to empirical investigations. This first

Table 1.1 *Three dominant theories in Comparative Politics, 1960–2020*

| Variable/theory | Structural functionalism | Rational choice | Democratic theory |
|---|---|---|---|
| Academic origin | Anthropology/ sociology | Economics | Philosophy |
| Main objective | Demonstrate systems similarity | Make analysis parsimonious | Prove universality of democratic norms |
| Principal focus | Structures | Human agency | Institutions |
| Preferred method | Qualitative | Quantitative | Variable |
| Critique | Difficult to operationalize | Oversimplification | Neglect of inherent normativity |

*Source:* Author

generation of comparativists sought inspiration in the Western intellectual tradition of thinking about the nature of social change (Shils 1963:11–12). The result was that functionalist theory became identified with the concept of modernization, which, in their view, treated democratic Western society as both the compass and the endpoint.

Structural functionalism initially generated a lot of enthusiasm, and some referred to it as the "new political science" or "the revolution in political science" (Easton 1969; Wiarda 2002). Those who were less excited soon identified weaknesses in the theory. Some pointed out the problematic nature of the theoretical scheme itself; others zeroed in on the contentious nature of the modernization concept. The former made two points. The first was the abstract nature of the theory and the difficulties related to operationalizing it. The second focused on the idea that structures are agents of their own, thus omitting the role that human agency plays in directing change through policy (Radcliffe Brown 1952; Durkheim 1953). The second line of criticism questioned the tendency in the theory to treat social change – represented by the modernization concept – as a cluster of internally compatible variables that "keep the system going" regardless of challenges to its legitimacy. Samuel P. Huntington (1965) was one of the first to point out that if one unpacks the concept and treats selective aspects of it, for example, institutions, one finds that modernization may strengthen instead of weaken traditional institutions and values, and rapid social change in one sphere may serve only to inhibit change in another. This critique also directed attention to the notion that tradition and modernity represent two mutually exclusive and functionally interdependent clusters of attributes. Rudolph and Rudolph (1967) showed in their research in India that in many instances "traditional" institutions and values may facilitate rather than impede social change. Modernization, therefore, cannot be equated simply with the destruction of tradition because the latter is not a prerequisite of modernization (Tipps 1973). From an African perspective, scholars such as Rotberg and Mazrui (1970) and Mbembe (2001) have criticized the Western development paradigm using a post-colonial constructivist argumentation.

As structural functionalism ran out of intellectual steam, the gap was filled in Africanist research by monographs focusing on the challenges of nation-building and bringing back human agency to the analysis. Although the literature was more varied, two accounts stand out as significant milestones in the first generation of Africanist political science. Aristide Zolberg (1966) devoted his research to the issues of creating political order and showed why West African leaders preferred to use single-party rule to hold their country together. Concern about liberal democracy was largely absent in the Comparative Politics literature at the time. The focus was on how the new states could be held together while embarking on a national development agenda. The early political breakdown of the Democratic Republic of Congo (then referred to as Congo-Kinshasa) and, soon thereafter, the civil war in Nigeria lent weight to the importance of research along these lines. An edited volume on the first post-independence elections in Tanzania in 1965 provided interesting insights into how political competition could be built into one-party rule by allowing two or more candidates to compete for the seat in each constituency (Cliffe 1967). This hybrid form of turning a primary into general election was later copied in other African countries, such as Kenya.

A second landmark study at the time focused on the cultural factors that helped in shaping the politics of national integration. Crawford Young's (1976) seminal book on the politics of cultural pluralism in Africa, based on his earlier research in Congo-Kinshasa, examined several African cases to show how modernization helped mobilize ethnic identities, especially in the growing urban centres across the continent. Much like the Rudolphs had argued with reference to India, Young empirically demonstrated that modernization was by no means a linear process but one characterized by contestation between communities appealing sometimes to modern and at other times to traditional features of society. In his comparison between societies in Asia and Africa, he concluded that the political challenge of dealing with cultural pluralism had similarities across the two regions. For example, he was the first to argue that countries such as India and Nigeria can be described not as nation-states but rather as state-nations whose prime task is to manage heterogeneity. Young's work was important in directing other Africanists at the time to focus on threats to state coherence and stability (e.g., Rothchild and Olorunsola 1983).

It is worth noting that when calls were made in the field for "bringing the state back in" (e.g., Evans et al. 1985) they coincided with the slowing down of research on the African state. As suggested earlier, it was especially pronounced in the years following independence when nation-building remained the outstanding challenge. The irony is that although structural functionalism relies on a systems theory to explain politics, the empirical examinations of African politics in the immediate post-independence period chose the role of the state as a more helpful guiding concept. This first attempt to incorporate African politics into a dominant theory, therefore, did not go far. The enthusiasm that the spurt had generated at first faded quite quickly when tested in the complex and at the time still largely uncharted terrain of African politics.

## 1.2.2   Rational Choice Theory

The second spurt in Comparative Politics was very much the opposite of the first. The ambition of structural functionalists was to include all possibly relevant variables into a single theory that could explain change at a high level of complexity. The nation-state (or state-nation) was the unit of analysis. Interest in human agency was nil. Instead, in functionalist theory, as noted earlier, structures took on the role of self-enforcing entities. The rational choice approach moved in the opposite direction. It eschewed complexity and took pride in offering parsimony, that is, the simplest possible explanation of a given policy puzzle.

Inspiration came from another long intellectual tradition in Western thinking dating back to Adam Smith. In his liberal market theory, individuals are perceived as innately ready to maximize their own utility. This simple formula is the core of the neo-liberal philosophy that emerged in the late 1970s and made its way into political science soon thereafter. Typically referred to as rational choice theory, it takes values out of the analytical equation by treating them as given and applicable to any cultural or national context. The injection of rational choice into the discipline spurred its growth in the direction of game theory and other similar models to analyse politics. It entered the comparative analysis of African politics in more modest ways. The most influential piece to pave the way for rational choice was probably the study by Robert Bates (1981) of markets and states in Africa. His book argues that most post-colonial government leaders in Africa favour urban consumers over rural agricultural producers, thereby limiting the growth potential of their economies. He shows how leaders in Kenya who had indeed accumulated land – and cultivated it – laid a stronger foundation for national development than their counterparts in Tanzania who were prevented by socialist policies from accumulating land and as a result tended to see their interest lie with urban consumers. It was not difficult to read on and between the lines that the growth of an indigenous middle class (or bourgeoisie) was viewed as a positive scenario.

The relative success of Bates's work and later studies in the same vein, for example, Posner (2005), in influencing the course of Comparative Politics prompted the growth of a broad alternative literature by African and expatriate neo-Marxists, pointing to the damage that these neo-liberal policy reforms were doing to African economies and society. This critical orientation had emerged already in opposition to modernization but gathered momentum among African and Africanist scholars as the World Bank and the International Monetary Fund demanded tough economic policy reforms of African governments in the late 1970s (Leys 1975; Amin 1976; Coulson 1982). Because rational choice theory was linked with international policy advice that ignored or downplayed local input, it never gained support in African academic circles. Instead, students in African universities in the 1980s were largely fed its neo-Marxist critique.

The neo-liberal analysis of African development, like that of the neo-Marxist, did not survive long. Both suffered from being out of touch with the socio-economic conditions in Africa. The former overestimated the magic of the market, the latter the transformative potential of a pre-capitalist society (Hyden 1980). Scepticism among political scientists reflected a critique along two lines. The first maintained that rational choice was too general, with parsimony easily becoming an end in and of itself, overlooking how structures and institutions confine agency (e.g., Young 1994; Mkandawire and Olukoshi 1995; Herbst 2000). The second came from pointing to the rich literature on the communal feature of African politics and its implications for human behaviour (e.g., Ekeh 1975; Wai 1987). Thus, the policy prescriptions derived from the use of a rational choice theory made little sense, and by the 1990s both theories had been abandoned or modified to the point where they exercised little influence on political science research in Africa. It was instead the flash of democratization, especially in Eastern Europe and Latin America, that started to attract comparativists, including those with an interest in Africa.

### 1.2.3   Democratic Theory

The third spurt using a general theory to explain politics is perhaps the most controversial because it is a tool not only for analysis but also for promoting a specific political agenda. Democratic theory is an outgrowth of Western philosophy and political experience. When it was put to life in comparative political analysis it drew on the writings of one of the most prominent theorists in the discipline, Robert Dahl (1971). What makes this attempt contested is that comparativists have embraced the notion of democracy as "the only game in town". By taking it for granted, comparative analysis has been made a matter of how well countries around the world play the game. This brash acceptance of democracy's normativity is present in measures of how closely countries adhere to a preconceived theoretical model derived from the experience of already mature democracies. The focus has been on the quality of a country's democratic institutions as they relate to holding free and fair elections, practising the rule of law, and respecting human rights. This approach has led to the creation of various governance indices that help analysts to quantitatively differentiate between countries in terms of their degree of democracy. Much of this was driven by the euphoria in the late twentieth century that democracy was seemingly gaining a hold in countries across the world. One of the most prominent scholars in the field of Comparative Politics, Huntington (1991), played an important role in setting the democratic research and policy agenda by labelling the process the "Third Wave of Democratization", which, unlike the two previous democratic waves in the twentieth century, had a global reach.

In an African perspective, much of what has been written by comparativists on democratization misses the point that effects of the Third Wave vary significantly not only between regions of the world but also among individual countries in each region. These differences rely both on the level of commitment to democratic values and on structural conditions. The prevailing institutional analysis puts too much emphasis on voluntarist human agency, ignoring the fact that choice and behaviour are also rooted in social formations or structures. This shortcoming is evident in the African cases where the democratic wave has not penetrated in the same way as it has done in Latin America and Eastern Europe. A major reason is that African countries lack the dynamic that comes from class-based social cleavages. Social formations in African countries are based not on relations of production but rather on relations of consumption. People are organized into communities that compete for control of how public resources are shared and distributed. As this book will discuss in greater detail, public institutions operate in a manner that is quite different from what democratic theory assumes. It should come as no surprise, therefore, that democratization has proved to be especially abstruse in the African region.

The problem with research driven by democratic theory has been its lack of attention to context. A review of institutional reforms in developing countries that include both politics and public administration concludes that these attempts have been largely unsuccessful because they have failed to alter underlying norms and values. The results of these reform efforts have been confined to redesign "on paper" rather than in practice (Andrews 2013). Another powerful signal of the limits of this research is the focus on "backsliding" (Bermeo 2016; Rakner 2018; Waldner and Lust 2018). While such backsliding may be significant in some regions of the world and noticeable not only in countries such as Turkey and Thailand but also in the United States, it is not a prime issue in Africa because of the limited penetration of democratic values in the first place. The African trajectory is different: the problem is not democracy in retreat but one still in demand. As Bratton and Housseou (2014) have demonstrated, people in Africa are still waiting for more democracy to be realized, a theme that is also at the centre of analysis in an edited overview of democratization in Africa (Lynch and VonDoepp 2020).

Levitsky and Ziblatt (2018) provide a recent overview of how democracies "die", that is, lose their legitimacy due to the subversion of existing institutions. This is a major research issue, but it is fore-most applicable to already developed democracies, not those that are still democratizing. In the latter, and it is especially true for Africa, the issue is not how democracy dies but why it is not growing. The answer lies in a closer examination of the conditions that favour or hinder the growth of democracy, such as the level of economic development, pre-dominant social cleavages, the presence of an indigenous middle class, or social mobility. These factors differentiate access to power and thus affect how politics is conducted. Africanists and other comparativists have reason to revisit the literature from the mid-twentieth century that argued that democracy does not arise or prevail in just any socio-economic conditions (Lipset 1959; Moore Jr 1966). Structures do matter!

## I.3   STUDYING DEMOCRACY BEYOND WAVES

It is increasingly clear that research on democratization, which has dominated Comparative Politics for some thirty years, faces a new and more challenging reality in the 2020s. Democratic theory no lon-ger offers the reassuring walls for a normal science where solving puzzles within that single framework is the most promising way for-ward. Anomalies are discovered in all regions of the world. We have reached a point of correction and renewal. This does not necessarily mean abandoning the concept of democracy but entails a fresh assess-ment of its role in development. Attention needs to be paid to those factors that so far have been largely omitted in the analysis guided by democratic theory. Democracy is a product of social and economic forces, and because societies differ along several dimensions, its pre-conditions vary. As noted earlier, this is not a new insight, but it needs to be brought back into comparative political analysis even if it is at the cost of cutting short the most recent period of attempted normal science in Comparative Politics.

Political development is a broader concept than democratiza-tion, although researchers in recent decades have treated the two as one and the same. The result is that comparative political analysis has been confined to narratives such as "democratic backsliding", "the rise of hybrid regimes" (Levitsky and Way 2010), and the coming of "a third wave of autocratization" (Lührmann and Lindberg 2019) rather than an impartial and open-ended analysis of which factors determine and shape political development. The fading or reversal of the Third Wave of Democratization ought to serve as enough of a wake-up call. First, backsliding or reversal is a logical consequence built into the wave metaphor. It should be no surprise, therefore, that democracy retreats much like it advances. Second, waves do not surge just anywhere at any time but are caused by natural forces. The same applies to democratization. It needs explanation with reference to factors in the socio-economic and political context. Third, waves do not necessarily hit with the same strength everywhere. Coastlines are not identical. It is important, therefore, to examine how variations in political development can be attributed to differences in the strength with which countries have been affected by the third wave. Fourth, much of democratic backsliding or reversal thinking is a figment of the mind. It results from an overestimation of the effects of the wave's initial democratic reforms. The euphoria that accompanied this turn of events was reflected in both expert evaluations and opinion surveys. It influenced everyone's subjective perceptions. In today's perspective, however, was the wave really such a transformative factor or was it more like a bump in an otherwise unbroken trajectory? Does the ongoing autocratization in some countries around the world merit the label of "wave"? These questions are increasingly relevant as countries across the world are faced with challenges to further democratic development.

The answer for comparativist research seems to lie in looking at democracy from the outside in, that is, studying the factors that determine its position in the broader political context as one regime type in competition with others. Experience in the last three decades has shown that there is nothing inevitable about democracy. It is not a given even in countries that are counted as "mature" democracies. More attention needs to be paid to what gives rise to democracy and what, other than voluntarist choices, keeps it going.

This book throws light on the viability of democracy and how the African conditions pose a challenge to the straightforward application of democratic theory. It begins with a discussion of the classical thesis in historical institutionalism that democracy is explained by socio-economic factors most famously expressed in Barrington Moore Jr's (1966) argument: "no bourgeoisie, no democracy". There is much more to how social formations affect the prospects of democracy, notably at what point in its historical development a specific country finds itself. This is especially relevant in the case of African countries where modernizing society has never advanced as far as in other regions and the conditions, therefore, are quite different. Those countries that have reached a high level of economic and social development have been able to do so by relying on a state capable of shaping society in its own democratic image. It has been critical in not only upholding territorial sovereignty but also integrating communities of people into a single entity, what today is generally referred to as the nation-state.

Many countries, however, have yet to reach the stage where national integration is complete. They are better described as state-nations because the state is still in the process of building or forming the nation. This is an issue in several countries around the world but is especially pertinent in Africa, where state formation was initiated but never completed by the European colonial powers. When African leaders, upon independence, decided that it was too risky to change the already established territorial borders, people were forced to co-exist in one and the same political unit even if they had nothing or little in common. Government leaders in Africa, therefore, continue to be preoccupied with trying to hold the national political community together, with immediate consequences for how democracy fits into their political agenda. The state is far from an independent public institution and rather a place for controlling rents, that is, public resources, that can be used to mitigate or neutralize political opposition, a condition that North et al. (2009) refer to as a "limited access order".

The history of African politics since independence, therefore, has been about the continuous tension between state and regime.

Political leaders have prioritized getting things done, notably pursuing a successful national development but have not been able to escape pressures, from both within and outside the region, to choose strategies based on respect for democracy and human rights. The chapters that follow will discuss how this tension manifests itself in state-nation relations, stabilizing political regimes, sustaining a functionable party system, and creating a viable public sphere – all critical factors in political development.

## 1.4    CONCLUSIONS

The problem with the three attempts at consolidating political analysis under a single overarching theory that have occurred in Comparative Politics is their teleological bent. They assume or describe trajectories that place Western society not only as the guide but also as the end-station for others. Democratic theory has been used in ways that are not very helpful for our understanding of what it means to democratize. The latter is not just a straightforward forward march to maximizing democratic values within a self-enforcing system. It involves carving out space within already existing systems of governance. Furthermore, its inherent positive normativity notwithstanding, political leaders governing systems in flux are forced to consider multiple and often conflicting values to keep political order and stability. To fathom the factors that determine choice and behaviour, attention must be paid to how macro-structures set the stage for what political actors do. It is necessary to focus the research lens on previously overlooked contextual variables. We are currently reaching a familiar point in Comparative Politics – the end of another brief period of normal science. What happened to structural functionalism and rational choice theory is now on the verge of befalling democratic theory. We are entering a period of evaluation and correction. It means greater uncertainty about what constitutes a dominant theory but also greater scope for bold conceptual redefinition and theoretical development.

# 2   How History Matters

2.1 ## 2.1   INTRODUCTION

The historical method of studying politics assumes that states and other political institutions are not made but grow out of preceding conditions, whether this is by way of constancy or change. To know what they are today, one needs to know their past and the forces that shaped their path to the present. The boundary between history and political science is not easy to define. As observational disciplines, both rely on narratives that place specific events in a wider temporal and spatial context. It happens quite often that what passes as political science is contemporary history. As this chapter attempts to show, it is hard to deny the place of history in the study of politics – or vice versa.

This is especially true when it comes to Africa, because its historical trajectory is different from that of other regions of the world. Situated in the periphery of the main developments in East Asia, the Middle East, and Western Europe, it fell behind when it came to such key determinants as the rise of a centralized state structure capable of shaping society in its own image and thereby transforming social life. Thus, the critical junctures that Westerners or the Chinese learn about in reading their history, for example, modernization and the rise of empire as patriotic achievements, have no immediate counterpart in African historiography. Understanding politics in Africa today involves appreciating its own anomalous past, first its isolation from the mainstream and later its subjugation to its drivers.

## 2.2 STRANDS OF HISTORICAL RESEARCH
## IN COMPARATIVE POLITICS

Historical insights come to Comparative Politics mainly through three strands of research. The first are studies of state formation. Charles Tilly's (1990) analysis of state formation in Europe over a period of thousand years (990–1990) shows the significance of two logics: that of coercion and that of capital. The first refers to how governments gain territorial control through the use of administration and monopoly of violence, the second to how human activities come together in economic networks by way of exchange, markets, credit, and transport. In a historical perspective these two ideal types of state formation produced different outcomes: the coercion-intensive path led to the rise of princedoms or monarchies, the capital-intensive to city-states. In the course of European history, a third form emerged, which combined the features of both ideal types and resulted in what Tilly calls "capitalized coercion". It incorporated cities and capital into national territories, which led to a more diverse but also effective use of public authority. Eventually, this third pattern prevailed, and states were institutionalized by combining effective authority, rich supply of capital, and a large population. Other scholars have carried out studies of state formation in other parts of the world and concluded that the European experience is not unique. Thus, Lieberman (2003) and Hui (2005) demonstrate how state formation in Eastern and South-eastern Asia followed a pattern similar to that of Europe.

The second strand has alerted comparativists to the importance of socio-economic transformations and their role in shaping politics. The most significant contribution in this tradition is Barrington Moore Jr's (1966) study of lords and peasants in the making of modern society. He makes two important points. The first is that modernization (or development) is not a gradual and peaceful process. Rather, it involves the use of violence between the main contenders – the rulers and the ruled. Depending on the class structure that accompanies development, Moore identifies three different paths by which modern society has been formed. The earliest is the "bourgeois revolution", in which violence removed the landed aristocracy and paved the way for a capitalist form of democracy as in Britain, France, and the United States. The second is the "revolution from above", in which the landowning elite retains control of the reins of power and through coercion develops a fascist dictatorship as in Germany and Japan. The third path to modernity is the "peasant revolution", which involves the overthrow of the landed aristocracy by a revolutionary peasantry. Russia and China constitute the principal cases in point. Theda Skocpol (1979) – like Tilly, a student of Moore – takes his scholarship further by arguing in a comparison of the revolutions in France, Russia, and China that they are the result of a combination of factors: state structure, class relations, and international forces. These forces rarely come together in a perfect-storm fashion, hence the rarity of great transformative events. An important sequitur to the comparative literature on social transformation is the argument made by Rueschemeyer et al. (1992) with reference to Europe, North America, Latin America, and the Caribbean that it is the working class rather than the bourgeoisie that has played the most significant role in securing democracy in capitalist countries.

The third strand is associated with the research done by Douglass North and his collaborators on the role of institutions in shaping economic performance (Levi 1989; North 1990; North et al. 2009). Their main point is that economic and political choices go together in ways that either limit or promote development. Advanced capitalist countries are effective because economic choices are made independently of partisan political interference. Actors perform in what the authors label an "open access order". The rest of the countries around the world are characterized by a limited access order, that is, a system in which political considerations determine economic choices. An example would be countries where a political leader has to "bribe" others to get his choice of policy approved. The problem with this approach is that it rests on a teleological way of interpreting choice. It becomes an echo of the modernization approach some sixty years ago.

Some comparativists are sceptical about the use of historical analysis, for example, because the causal relations tend to be imprecise. This criticism is valid although not necessarily strong enough to delegitimize comparative historical analysis altogether. This is certainly true for those historical institutionalists who focus their study on key events – "critical junctures" that lay the foundation for subsequent institutionalization, referred to as "path dependency". A persuasive example using this approach is the comparative study by Ruth Berins Collier and David Collier (1978) of how the labour movement in four Latin American countries was incorporated by political parties or state institutions. They treat this incorporation as a critical juncture that paved the way for lasting but different political development trajectories in these four countries.

Historical explanations in Comparative Politics, however, do not abound. Dominant theorizing starts from the premise that political systems are already settled hierarchies of authority. In that perspective, the study of politics gets decoupled from its historical roots. The cost of such decoupling, however, is evident in the literature on the emerging challenges to democracy around the world (Schedler 2006; Bogaards 2009). Democracy has roots in society, and where these roots are not evident, the explanation must focus on its underlying conditions. In the African case, this means examining not only its colonial past but also its precolonial legacies.

## 2.3   CHALLENGES OF STUDYING PRE-COLONIAL AFRICA

Unlike the states in Europe and Asia that benefitted from a literary tradition and thus sources that could be cited to construct – or reconstruct – hegemonic narratives, pre-colonial African societies lacked indigenous written sources of their past. Apart from glimpses provided by transient visitors, little was known about these societies. The information available came from oral history sources and was typically confined to a given community and its contacts with neighbouring groups. An important study that early on made its way into Comparative Politics was the classification and comparison of African political systems by Fortes and Evans-Pritchard (1940). It came to serve as an influential reference in the comparative volume on the politics of the developing areas that helped in laying the ground for the field (Almond and Coleman 1960). Further attention to pre-colonial politics and state formation in Africa has been scant in the discipline. One reason is the difficulty of obtaining sources, another its perceived irrelevance for post-colonial Africa.

Africa's pre-colonial past, however, is indeed important beyond the boundaries of the discipline of history. During the colonial period, Africa's historiography was dominated by Europeans who saw the region from their own external perspective. The period after independence has been devoted to correcting timelines and other key aspects of these colonial accounts. This movement was directed by Kenneth Dike, a Nigerian historian, and supported by nationalist leaders in Africa such as Kwame Nkrumah of Ghana and Leopold Sedar Senghor of Senegal (Nwaubani 2000). Rewriting the history of Africa's own past, therefore, has been and remains a political project with implications for narratives and interpretations. There is obviously no objective account in history; each lends itself to multiple interpretations. For this reason, I have chosen to also include accounts produced by scholars associated with Kyoto University in Japan.

Their research is interesting and relevant here because it transcends the limits of the main Western strands of theorizing about human development. Following in the tradition of one of the pioneers at the university's Institute for Research in Humanities, Shumpei Ueyama (1966), Japanese researchers have advocated an approach to human history that involves multiple paths based on the ecological conditions of each major region of the world. This regionalized approach to political economy provides a more open-ended perspective for interpreting the relevance of the pre-colonial roots for contemporary politics in Africa.

## 2.4    UNFULFILLED STATE DEVELOPMENT

In a comparative ecological perspective, as Ueyama shows in his work, the most significant historical transformation was the creation of agrarian society because it laid the foundation for a full-fledged state and a stratified society. This revolutionary event denotes a series of measures that radically changed the social landscape, notably the mass production of grain based on irrigation systems and the creation of urban centres, both of which fostered the rise of a ruling class and centralized state power based on institutions such as bureaucracy, a standing army, the legal system, letters, and religion. It facilitated the mobilization of people by the state to develop agricultural production, for example, through public works to construct and manage irrigation facilities.

This agrarian revolution, characterized by large-scale irrigation agriculture and the mass production of cereals, first took place around 4000 BC, leading to the rise of ancient civilizations like that in Mesopotamia. This significant development in the production system was accompanied by the emergence of a multi-layered social structure, which eventually required a state to coordinate and control society. Karl Wittfogel (1957) developed the concept of "hydraulic civilization" to describe societies whose agriculture was dependent upon large-scale waterworks for irrigation and flood control. By 2000 BC the agrarian revolution had paved the way for the formation of agrarian societies not only in the Middle East and the Mediterranean regions but also in other drylands such as northern China and western India. The agrarian civilization gradually advanced into forest lands including northern Europe, South-east Asia, and Japan, where the creation of states can be observed in the early or mid-first millennium AD. From the late eighteenth century to the late nineteenth century, the industrial revolution took place first in Britain and other parts of Europe and then in Japan. By this point in time, the effective state control of peasant production based on stratified and sedentary farming communities was prevalent in Europe, Asia, and the

Americas. Their farming system was characterized by grain-centred agriculture with standardized staple crops. The system, for example, laid the foundation in much of Western Europe for a feudal type of land tenure system, which characterized the region prior to the industrial revolution.

Africa has had its share of state systems – kingdoms and empires, for example, Songhai, Ashanti, Bunyoro-Kitara, and Zulu, to mention some of the more important (see, e.g., Ajayi and Crowder 1976). Even though these were powerful and interacted with Arabs and Europeans as equals, they never developed into agrarian states. In his book on state-making in ancient Mesopotamia, James Scott (2017) offers multiple clues to the origin of agrarian states as well as their relations to surrounding non-state people made up of mobile hunters-and-gatherers, pastoralists, and shifting cultivators. Like Ueyama, he pays special attention to the emergence of grain cultivation on a large scale, which eventually paved the way to state formation. Early states, not only in Mesopotamia but also in Egypt and China, were all dependent on the concentration of grain production and manpower. Scott emphasizes that early states were often short-lived and unstable, as it was difficult to tame and subordinate producers who were originally free and could depend on mobile and dispersed subsistence strategies rather than the mono-cropping associated with fixed-field cultivation. Although he does not mention Africa there is a striking resemblance between his description of non-state people and rural dwellers in pre (and post)-colonial Africa.

Pre-state polities like the chiefdom (as the extended form of a clan society) are characterized by reciprocal exchange, while agrarian state systems rely on plunder and redistribution of peasant surplus products by a king or a feudal lord (Karatani 2014). Clan society, in Scott's view, is not a backward form of social formation but an ingenious invention to prevent inequality and the eventual formation of a state. Unlike the despotic ruler of a state, the tribal chief cannot hold absolute power. His position is secure only as far as he shares his wealth with others, thus mitigating the emergence of an ever-growing gap in wealth and power in society. A supra-community or alliance of tribal or clan groups may be formed, but the sub-groups retain a definite degree of independence. Thus, a clan society (or chiefdom) is not necessarily one that has failed to form a state structure but rather a system that has been able to avoid state formation (Karatani 2014:9).

As Tsuruta (2020) notes, like Scott, Karatani criticizes the prevailing notion that human beings inherently favour a sedentary mode of life and a status as state subjects. Although from different perspectives, both stress the difficulty of "capturing" people who have their own alternative subsistence activities and modes of exchange. Their point is relevant for analysing the formation and dissolution of polities in Africa, past and present. Africa is today the only region of the world where pre-capitalist modes of reciprocal exchange have survived as major determinants of human livelihoods and national development. In Asia, Europe, and the Americas, agrarian state systems developed over a long period of time. Equally important, these developments took place before there was an attempt to democratize politics. By the end of the nineteenth century, Africa was without developed indigenous state systems that could propel societies forward in the same way as in other regions of the world. It fell upon European countries to establish a system of colonial rule to fill this historical vacuum. So, why did African societies south of the Sahara never develop long-lasting centralized agrarian states or a persistent subordination of the peasants?

## 2.5   WHY AFRICA FELL SHORT IN STATE DEVELOPMENT

The origin of agriculture is not the same as the origin of agrarian society as is evident, for example, in the contribution of savannah cultivars to the development of agriculture around the Mediterranean that gave birth to the great ancient civilizations of Mesopotamia and Egypt. According to Sasuke Nakao (1966), Africa is home to one of the oldest forms of agriculture and important domestic plants including millets, sorghum, sesame, and cow peas. Savannah agriculture in Africa was for a long time as advanced as any other agricultural system in the world but it gradually lost its position, the main reason being that the savannah societies did not go through an agrarian revolution. They were never transformed by indigenous social forces that would produce a state as a driver of change. Tsuruta (2020) provides three reasons for the absence of such a trajectory in Africa: (1) the limited influence of other civilizations, (2) the ruler reliance on trade, and (3) the "extensive" way of life.

### 2.5.1  *Little Influence from Other Civilizations*

Sub-Saharan Africa's geographical position in relation to the other civilizations and its natural environment have been decisive factors in shaping its history. It is close to the Mediterranean, where the "ancient civilizations" developed. Some of the early polities in sub-Saharan Africa borrowed economic and religious ideas from both the Islamic and Christian civilizations. It was only northern Ethiopia, as a periphery of Mediterranean-Islamic civilization, however, that developed a polity close to an agrarian state, with a formal bureaucracy, local aristocracy, and heavy taxation of peasants (McCann 1995). The introduction of ox-ploughs allowed for grain cultivation on a larger scale,[1] a practice that is still in use in present-day Ethiopia. Except for this case, however, polities (mainly established under the impact of Islam) never nurtured a lasting state structure. Early Islamic influences were later largely but not wholly replaced by those of Western Europe, which through colonization came to have a greater impact on the continent's socio-economic structure.

External influences were slow to have an impact upon African societies in pre-colonial times. In his comparison of civilizations in Africa and South-East Asia, Kakeya (2018:206–10) divides the sub-Saharan region into three major parts: Sahel, Swahili, and Inland

---

[1] It is worthy of note that Ethiopia was the only pre-colonial society in sub-Saharan Africa that had a significant tradition of map-making and plough cultivation, both of which are related to the effective control and appropriation of land (Herbst 2014:38–40).

Africa. Located in the southern periphery of the Sahara, Sahel has been deeply involved in trans-Saharan trade with the Arab world. The Swahili coastal area in East Africa has been shaped by the wider Indian Ocean trading networks. Sahel and Swahili, as culturally coherent areas, were formed through these trading interactions with the outside world. Inland Africa, on the other hand, remained largely isolated from such external influences.

On the East African coast, over the centuries, with a constant migration of Arabs and Persians, the Islamic urban way of life became an integral part of Swahili culture, which flourished in port towns from the thirteenth century or in some places even earlier. In contrast to the Sahel, however, the influence of the Swahili civilization was largely limited to a narrow strip of the coast, probably because of the unfavourable and drier environment of the hinterland (Connah 1987:176). Thus, Swahili political organizations remained largely as city-states based on trade and had only a limited impact on inland agricultural communities.

It is most likely only the Sahel (along with forest and coastal areas south of it) that could have produced fully fledged states to match those of other agrarian societies. This semi-arid area south of the Sahara saw the rise and fall of "empires", each in control of a wide territory. Numerous polities emerged in the area from the eighth century until the time immediately before European colonization. The Sahelian civilizations, however, were repeatedly subject to invasion by external forces that prevented a continuous and cumulative historical development. The Ghana Empire (circa 8C–11C) was conquered by the Almoravids (a faction of Berber nomads) invading from the north. It was succeeded by Mali (circa 13C–16C) and Songhai (circa 15C–16C) Empires, both of which, like their predecessor, flourished thanks to trans-Saharan trade (Diop 1976). Although historical materials are scant, it seems that the Songhai Empire promoted grain production along the Niger River by making waterways and settling slaves captured in warfare. The empire, however, eventually collapsed due to the invasion of Moroccan forces (Niane 1984). Tsuruta (2020) believes that the Songhai Empire may have subjugated agricultural communities in some spots but not over a wide area nor over a long period of time. A tradition of agriculture, language, and family system at the grassroots continued to exist but the imperial political institutions did not. These pre-modern African polities have had virtually nothing to do with the trajectory of state formation in modern Africa. The Atlantic slave trade initiated by Europeans and their eventual colonization ended any endogenous development of local civilizations.

### 2.5.2   *Ruler Reliance on Trade*

Power in the pre-modern African polities rested more often on control of trade than on agricultural production. With a sparse population scattered across the open savanna or the tropical forest, it was easier for these polities to tax long-distance as well as local trade (Connah 1987; Iliffe 1995). By examining several of them, Coquery-Vidrovitch (1978) concludes that traditional African societies had a dual social structure: a power elite based on long-distance trade and an autonomous subsistence village economy. She asserts that the revenue of pre-colonial polities mostly came from either long-distance trade or warfare booties rather than levies collected from villagers. Rural Africa in pre-colonial times was also unique in the absence of land alienation by an upper class. To quote, "in Black Africa, the sovereign exploited the neighboring peoples, not his own subjects" (Coquery-Vidrovitch 1988:57). Jack Goody (1971), who argued that feudalism never took root in Sahelian agriculture, attributed this to its lack of technology. Despite the contacts the Sahelian societies had with the Mediterranean civilizations, they never invented or adopted modes of production aimed at enhancing specialization. Cultivation instead relied on rudimentary hand tools, which limited the area that could be planted and the level of productivity that could be reached.

The economy of Sahelian empires and kingdoms was geographically based on the rule over scattered "desert ports of trade" and, as Shimada (2006) notes, in some cases the control of mines. There is little evidence of intensive agriculture in pre-colonial West Africa except possibly for irrigation based on natural flooding as practised in the inland Niger Delta and Lake Chad (Connah 1987:111; Shimada 2006). Even the use of manure was a rarity. Given the importance of trade and warfare, raising livestock (camels, donkeys, and cattle as pack animals and horses for cavalry) was the most important preoccupation. The lack of priority in transforming land tenure and land use for the purpose of greater productivity meant that any attempt at state-building rested on a weak foundation (Nakao 1966).

### 2.5.3   An Extensive Way of Life

Inland Africa is interesting in comparison with the Sahel and Swahili civilizations because it was much less influenced by outside forces. Social change was marked by migration and the conflicts that arose as people claimed new land. Rarely did these lead to greater social stratification and enhanced state-building. There were some exceptions, however, especially in what we today refer to as the Great Lakes region. Following the conquest by pastoral groups, these societies produced a system of social stratification that Maquet (1961) labelled feudal with specific reference to the Kingdom of Rwanda. Lemarchand (1970) further elaborated the analysis of Rwandan society, reaching the conclusion that it was being governed centrally but through reciprocal exchanges between the lords and their underlings that at least in pre-colonial times served to modify tension and conflict. Drawing on Kopytoff's (1989) argument about the African frontier, Kakeya (2018), however, views Inland Africa as an "internal frontier", in contrast to the forestlands in South-East Asia, which he describes as an "external frontier" open to maritime trade networks. People living in Inland Africa engaged in frequent settlement relocation and what Kakeya (ibid) terms an "extensive way of life", a contrast to the "intensive" production systems that originated in agrarian societies. With low population density, Africans utilized their surrounding environment extensively by combining shifting cultivation with fishing or hunting and gathering. The village economy was largely self-sufficient, and the salient feature of village society was the levelling mechanism based on the norm of reciprocity. The basic type of social formation was a loose federation of small chiefdoms. In some cases, these chiefdoms developed into "kingdoms" with a wider territory (often based on long-distance trade), but each village's subsistence economy was retained.

Kakeya and Kopytoff demonstrate the highly fluid nature of group formation in Inland Africa, driven foremost by the constant ebb and flow of polities. Attempts to form a state-like structure were typically followed by the movement of residents to escape from state formation. Scott's (2009) argument about "escape agriculture" is helpful for understanding the migrations of people in Inland Africa. Referring to the "stateless" hill tribes in the mountainous areas of South-East Asia, Scott argues that these people deliberately selected certain farming systems and crops to "escape" from the mighty arms of the lowland states based on wet rice cultivation. Shifting cultivation and the adoption of "escape crops" such as sweet potato, cassava, and maize were particularly important strategies employed to avoid control by lowland agrarian states. These are the same crops that have dominated small-scale agriculture in Africa to this day. The arms of the state in Inland Africa were never developed enough to extend control over large populations and the notion of "escape agriculture" is still relevant. African peasant farmers see little value in the state and give priority to growing subsistence rather than commercial crops that can be taxed by the government. Research by Hyden (1980), Hart (1982), and Richards (1985) demonstrates the fallacy of agricultural policy in African countries, usually prompted by international funding, that assumes the same power of the state as in societies that have already gone through an agrarian revolution.

## 2.6   EFFECTS OF MISSING THE AGRARIAN REVOLUTION

The agrarian state system, despite its oppressive nature, encouraged new political dynamics. It was at least in part driven by a gradual technological development from subsistence to mixed and eventually commercial farming. Modern society has a lot to thank agrarian revolution. The account in the previous section has shown how sub-Saharan Africa has become part of the modern world without first passing through an agrarian revolution. Unlike what happened elsewhere in the twentieth century, colonialism forced rural Africa to take on modernization without its own agrarian society foundation.

The colonial powers tried to modernize agriculture in Africa. Because of elusive, dispersed, and self-sufficient communities of cultivators, pastoralists, and agro-pastoralists, as well as hunters-and-gatherers who frequently moved from one place to another, the process of incorporating these people into a modern state system and economy has proved to be difficult and full of twists and turns (e.g., von Freyhold 1979). There is no single response among the region's peasants. They are fickle, some engaging with the state and market, others preferring to stay out of such engagement. This ambivalence is in sharp contrast with most South-east Asian farmers who in recent decades have fully embraced agricultural commercialization at the expense of traditional socio-economic systems. Even though the African countryside has also been commercialized, its prime feature is the co-existence of commercialized farmers and subsistence peasants in the same social setting (Tsuruta 2020).

The international community has approached the agricultural development issues in Africa with its own experience in mind. Donor governments have done their best to encourage mono-crop regimes in place of the inter-crop systems that characterize rural Africa. Furthermore, they have supported the consolidation of land holdings to facilitate a transition to a more productive form of agriculture. Complementing this move has been a policy of encouraging private land tenure. Much of this has been pursued with little attention to local conditions, notably the absence of an agrarian basis,[2] the very

---

[2] The term "agrarian bias" has so far been used by development experts to mean the preference for the agricultural sector over the development of the industrial sector (e.g., Hodge 2007:262–72).

fundament on which donor and government policies in Africa are pursued (Hyden et al. 2020).

The result is that governance in African countries tends to be bifurcated. One part of the system relies on private land tenure rights enforced by government and the funding from institutions supported by the international community. It is the formal system whose features and quality are assessed in global indices. The other part is made up of the informal institutions that grow out of local conditions, for example, mutual aid groups, patron–client relations, and local faith communities, whether devoted to gods or spirits. These two systems – the formal and the informal – are more often out of tune with each other rather than being mutually supportive. As two comparativists noted with reference to democratization in Latin America, informal institutions are not necessarily harmful for democracy (Helmke and Levitsky 2006). This type of institutions in Latin America, however, are lodged in societies that have already gone through an agrarian transformation. There is a state acting in a sovereign manner to restrict the space within which informal institutions can operate. Such is not the case in African countries where informal institutions continue to enjoy their own sovereignty and remain largely independent of the formal ones. Whether it is clientelism, mutual aid, or belief systems, these informal institutions enjoy a level of legitimacy that state institutions lack, a point that Ekeh (1975) made long ago and others have later confirmed (e.g., MacLean 2010). These informal institutions tend to have a greater influence on both policy and politics than the decisions that are taken by government and other public institutions. African politics, therefore, have features and qualities that are easily ignored without recognition of its anomalous path to the present.

## 2.7 CONCLUSIONS

As this chapter has tried to demonstrate, human efforts to manage the tension between the past and the present is at the core of how societies develop. This is true not only for those countries or regions with a rich history that has already been fully explored. It also applies to countries in Africa whose history has been under-researched but is crucial for understanding its contemporary challenges, including how to advance democratic development. Much of the historical legacy in Africa is informal, which means that efforts by state institutions – often boasted by international donor partners – tend to fall short of reaching official policy goals. Producers on the land escape by focusing on subsistence rather than commercial crops, those in the urban areas by relying on unofficial rules. State control is ineffective because the dominant cultural orientation is to evade the long arm of the state. The idea of a social contract between the ruler and the ruled has been very hard to nurture in post-colonial Africa. Instead, development in the region has relied on intermittent and flexible institutional arrangements with direct consequences for how society is governed. This is perhaps the most significant way that history keeps influencing the present.

# 3    Relevance of Social Formations

Social formation is a concept derived from Marxist theory of how capitalism penetrates pre-capitalist modes of production and in the process changes them forever. It is not commonly used in Comparative Politics, but it has a special relevance to the study of African politics because it is marked by the tension between the past and the present, especially the extent to which colonialism has penetrated Africa's pre-capitalist structures.

The concept had a more pronounced presence in the early days of the field. Sixty years ago, social formations were an integral part of comparing political regimes. Seymour Martin Lipset set the tone for this research orientation with two contributions, an article devoted to analysing what he termed the "social requisites" of democracy (1959) and, the following year, a monograph with the title *Political Man* (1960). Both argued that democracy was a product of modernization. Lipset suggested that modernization is one of several factors shaping democracy, but many who interpreted his work were inclined to see a more deterministic relation between the two. A few years later, Barrington Moore Jr (1966) provided an ambitious interpretation of how the social origins of democracy and dictatorship are determined by the social forces at play in the transition from agrarian to industrial society in six key countries around the world. Another influential publication was the edited volume on social cleavage structures, party systems, and voter alignment in Europe (Lipset and Rokkan 1967). It spurred research on political parties, much of which will be discussed in Chapter 6.

Since then, political sociology has given way to political economy and a greater focus on institutional analysis. Qualitative historical analysis has been increasingly replaced by statistics and quantitative analysis. Samuel Huntington (1968) was pioneering institutional analysis as an alternative approach to the one founded in political sociology. Douglass North (1990) and later Adam Przeworski et al. (2000) bridged the transition to the dominance of a political economy outlook that has been mainstream in the 2000s. Today the social basis of politics is rarely problematized in comparative political analysis. For example, the institutions that underpin democracy are treated as viable in any socio-economic condition. It is in the context of such theorizing that African politics becomes a conundrum. Because of the relatively recent colonial experience, its socio-economic foundation compared to other regions of the world is different. This chapter lays out this difference and sets the African condition in its wider political economy context.

## 3.2  MAINSTREAM POLITICAL ECONOMY

The bulk of comparative political analysis today rests on the self-assured premise that the institutional landscape is stable and that deviations can be handled within a single dominant theoretical model. Such is certainly the case with studies of democratization that have flourished on the premise that democracy is "the only game in town". The macro perspective on social and economic conditions is replaced in these studies by a disaggregated statistical examination of people's individual socio-economic status (Beetham 1994; Coppedge 2012). Gone is the "big picture". This reductionist approach shrinks the analysis to a technical puzzle aimed at interpreting the symbolic meaning of numbers. The roots of democracy are of no interest or consequence.

The reality that is disaggregated in comparative democratic analysis is a replica of a society that has gone through an agrarian as well as industrial revolution. Interest groups are organized accordingly and constitute the basis for the formation of political parties.

Political life is set along a right–left spectrum. Party systems tend to be stable even if there may be changes in the individual party composition. For example, in dominant two-party systems there may at times be movements of support to a third party, although the latter typically does not become more than a temporary tiebreaker.

Omitted in this research is attention to how these parties have come about and why the party system in these countries has persisted over long time. Some of it may be explained by the civic trust that the democratic system itself has helped generate but it is also a product of the relative institutional stability that occurs where political action is grounded in the economic production process. It encourages compromises and readiness to accept sub-optimal policy outcomes, a key ingredient of democratic politics. It is easy to overlook the significance of this variable when the analysis is only centred on the quality of democratic institutions. The cost of overlooking the socio-economic dynamics has become increasingly obvious as democracy is backsliding in the face of emerging populist forms of politics.

African politics has not really been effectively organized along the lines of economic interests. The colonial powers tried to encourage the institutional fundament of such politics, but it was incomplete at the time of independence. There was the beginning of a trade union movement and the first stages of a consumer and producer cooperative movement (Coleman 1965). The political leadership in the new African states came largely out of these movements. Once in power, however, the leaders introduced legislation to ban or reduce the powers of these non-state organizations. Because there was no independent African middle class with capital to influence development, the post-independence political organizations never took on a "class" character. The neo-Marxist scholarship that flourished in the 1970s and onwards was more ideological than analytical. It imputed too uncritically the exploitation and oppression on the continent to the presence of social classes similar to what would be found in Western society (e.g., Arrighi and Saul 1973; Leys 1975; Gutkind and Wallerstein 1976). Not surprisingly, its influence waned quickly. By assuming the hegemonic nature of colonialism, these neo-Marxist authors downplayed the role of indigenous African social formations in the same way as advocates of neo-liberal theory in the decade that followed.

## 3.3  AFRICAN FORMATIONS

Unlike production systems in agrarian and industrial societies, African agriculture is organized not to enhance productivity but primarily to satisfy consumption needs. It avoids specialization in favour of diversification. Livelihoods rely on individual endeavour, but when they fall short of human needs, sharing occurs within informally constituted communities of consumption. In Africa, people form such communities based on kin, gender, religion, or location. The rich join the poor. Social cleavages, therefore, are not between upper and lower classes but between communities of consumption relying on primary criteria of social organization. Politics is based on rivalling identities rather than competing interests generated by market forces and state policies.

The analysis of African social formations has been sullied by a series of Eurocentric misconceptions. The notion of "primitive society", while recognizing that society is held together through social reproduction (Kuper 1988), creates the impression that African society conditions are somehow inferior to those of agrarian or industrial society. Another concept that has limited the expansion of interest in Africa's social formations is "tribal society". Like yet another one – "traditional society" – it portrays African social structures as doomed to destruction by a Western-led modernization machine (Gutkind 1970). While "primitive society" and "tribal man" may have disappeared from the literature, other misconceptions have taken their place. As suggested earlier, neo-Marxist writers have done their own damage to our understanding of the African condition by imposing a global frame of class analysis that ignores the empirical realities. Although the colonial powers did their best to overturn indigenous social formations, they never really succeeded in their ambition.

Thus, two decades after countries had become politically independent, one observer described the situation in West Africa in the following terms:

> In the case of West African agriculture, the dominant form of labor is not done for wages, but by a family worker farming on his own account. This farmer is not free from complex social ties: He may be embedded in associations derived from membership in a descent group, and he is most certainly working alongside his wife and children in a setting that is domestic. He may be a sharecropper, splitting his product with a landlord who does not "own" the land and who may be a senior kinsman. He may be working on a settlement regulated by the government or a religious order. All of these are variations of peasant farming, and they still predominate (Hart 1982:117–18).

Hart's characterization confirms the persistence of social formations that have not been subordinated to the commands of an agrarian state. Local variations can be found in other parts of the sub-Saharan region. For example, Goody (1971:24–25) shows that the origin of these forms does not lie in differences in mercantile activities. As discussed in Chapter 2, trade was highly organized in both pre-colonial East and West Africa. Whether societies were kingdoms or stateless, barter had given way to more complex forms of exchange. The origin instead can be found in technology (or perhaps better said – lack of it). Unlike Eurasian societies in the Bronze Age, Africa never adopted the plough that enabled a substantial rise in agricultural productivity, which in turn meant a greater surplus for the maintenance of special crafts, the growth of differences in wealth and lifestyles, and the expansion into urban-based developments. Furthermore, this process stimulated the move to fixed holdings and away from shifting agriculture, with the result that the availability of arable land decreased and its value increased.

Pre-colonial Africans made little or no use of mechanical tools, even quite elementary ones. For example, animal power, which pulled the plough in Asia and Europe, was not applied for agricultural use, a prime reason being that the wheel, despite the existence of an iron-smelting technology, was never adopted for farming purposes. The lack of the wheel also limited the possibilities for water control. Irrigation existed in pre-colonial Africa, but it never raised agricultural production to significant surpluses. Hoe farming by men or women prevailed across the region in those days.

It can of course be argued that the reason why there was no agricultural transformation like in Europe and Asia is that there was more than enough land to cultivate for everyone. Land use intensification, therefore, was not a necessity. This had implications for how households and families were structured, as Boserup (1965) convincingly argued. In sparsely populated regions where shifting cultivation is used, men do little farm work. Because work falls on the shoulders of women – and their children – marriage is often polygynous. Furthermore, marriage is a deal where the family of the groom pays bride-wealth to the family of the girl. This transaction differs from what happens in societies where agriculture is more advanced, men do the work, marriages are monogamous, and women tend to be valued only as mothers. Here, the marriage transaction goes the other way: a dowry is paid by the girl's family to that of the bridegroom, typically interpreted as a contribution to the livelihood of a nuclear household.

Goody has elaborated on this difference that sets Africa apart from Eurasia by showing that inheritance patterns also vary. Because parental property in Africa is shared in the marriage transaction, wives can make no claim to the husband's property upon his death. Instead, such property is transmitted only to members of his own clan or lineage. Women are not entitled to share in the property of their fathers or mother's brothers, even when they are members of the same unilineal descent group (Goody 1976:6–8). This lateral transfer of property to brothers and sons but not daughters stand in contrast to Eurasia where the plough and use of irrigation have allowed for more advanced forms of cultivation. Here the transmission is vertical, that

is, within monogamous families allowing both male and female children to have access to the estate of their deceased parents.

These historical differences between Africa and other regions
of the world had consequences for social organization and social differentiation. As we have shown in Chapter 2, there were differences
in wealth, but stratification was due not to capital but to labour.
Chiefs and other potentates owed their power to political office,
not to being landlords owning land on which others were tenants.
They ruled through and over people, not land. Polygyny was used to
cement social bonds across families and households. The Kingdom of
Eswatini (Swaziland) where almost every family is somehow related
to the king is perhaps the best example of how this pre-colonial legacy lives on in national politics in Africa today. Demonstrating the
number of followers is more significant than claims to territory. It is
also instructive that in northern Ethiopia, where farmers did adopt
plough cultivation, land took on a considerable economic value. The
use of marriage transactions to maintain social status, like in Europe
and Asia, led to forms of social stratification not found elsewhere on
the continent. It may be argued, therefore, that Ethiopia (certainly
the northern part) is African in a geographical but not a social sense.

Elsewhere on the continent, even in centralized kingdoms,
social organization was fluid and rarely based on differences in land-
holding. Land was owned communally by a lineage group though
exploited by smaller family units. There was enough land to hold
some of it in fallow and no one had to beg on their knee to have
access to land. Sharing food was a principle of honour for the already
wealthy. For these reasons, African societies did not develop feudal
patterns of social organization characterized by serfdom or peonage.
Slavery was widespread but yielded only minor payoffs. Clientship
existed but the subjection associated with such transactions involved
cattle, as in Rwanda, or political rights, for example, to collect tribute or taxes. In fact, as discussed in Chapter 2, income from tax-
ing trade and gifts from traders contributed more to the income
and status of rulers in pre-colonial Africa than rent or tribute from

agricultural activities ever did (Goody 1976:104–12). It is worth noting that social and political violence in post-colonial Africa has not
really been directed against the upper strata of society. Peasants
have risen against indigenous rulers only in Ethiopia, Rwanda, and
Zanzibar, where marriage rules were meant to isolate the ruling
caste. Elsewhere, conflicts causing civil violence have typically been
between groups organized along communal or religious lines. These
facts clearly show that African societies never produced a coherent
"peasant class", which was normally created in other regions through
a long history of subjugation of smallholder cultivators by an upper
class controlling the state. It is no surprise that in a Marxist perspective, as one scholar writes about Tanzania, "politics in the periphery
remain fragile and masses disorganized" (Shivji 2021:9).

Social formations attributable to the persistence of pre-agrarian
modes of production continue to be important determinants of politics in Africa. This does not mean that conditions are stagnant. As
Sara Berry (1993) notes, no condition in Africa is permanent. Several
factors outside the local context are nowadays influencing what happens on the land. These factors deserve further elaboration not only
by historians but also by comparativist political scientists with an
interest in transcending the limitations associated with a Western
perspective on the region or the generalities of global theory, be it
liberal or Marxist. To fully appreciate the influence of Africa's social
formations and how they shape contemporary politics, the following
two features are of special importance: (1) they are diverse and flexible, and (2) they are self-regulating.

### 3.3.1   Diversity and Flexibility

African producers constantly adjust their livelihood to the shifting environment through migration, changes in farming systems, and/or the
incorporation of other subsistence strategies such as hunting, gathering, and livestock herding. In recent decades, adjustment includes supplementary income through wage labour, even office work. Diversity,
multiplicity, and mobility continue to characterize livelihoods in

Africa, in stark contrast to those in agrarian and industrial societies, which are marked by uniformity and sedentariness. Attempts by both colonial and independent governments to turn people into producers of one thing instead of simultaneously spreading themselves into multiple livelihood sources have failed. The norms of local society continue to permeate livelihoods, giving rise to an extensive informal sector that escapes the arms of the state and the sanctions of the market.

People in African societies, therefore, are not caught in permanent structures reflecting the presence of a singularly powerful state or market. In agrarian societies, the state controls the production systems of the peasantry as a subordinate class, hence the presence of uniform farming systems and livelihood patterns. In contrast, in sub-Saharan Africa peasant communities have remained largely autonomous, dispersed, and without a social stratification based on individual land ownership. Their production patterns have been dictated primarily by local ecology and consumption needs rather than decrees by state institutions. The argument is similar to Alexander Chayanov's (1966) point about the Russian peasantry in the early twentieth century, but there is a significant difference. His theory was based on consumption within single households. In rural Africa, however, it is shared consumption among several interlinked households that dictates production patterns. A given unit of production is not necessarily the same as the unit of consumption. Foods and other goods are shared and redistributed among different households through which social relations are reproduced and their production level is determined. The political economy of rural Africa is one of sharing. In a study of the Tongwe people in western Tanzania, Makoto Kakeya (1986), for example, demonstrates how, despite inequality in crop production, food consumption of each household is eventually evened out through the active sharing of foods. Another researcher, Yuko Sugiyama (1987), found a similar levelling mechanism among the Bemba people of northern Zambia. They make the point that the extensive mode of production that characterizes most of rural Africa is quite different from what is found in other regions of the world where the mentality of raising productivity on privately owned farms prevails and an ensuing socio-economic inequality is ubiquitous. Because cultivation of the land tends to be modest and carried out within the limits of what nature permits, the African peasant is not like the farmer in agrarian or industrial society who specializes to enhance productivity and income. Instead, as Kakeya (1986) notes, he is a "generalist" manager of his environment, both physical and social, combining the two to get enough to subsist and share with others in the community of consumption of which he is a member.

### 3.3.2   Self-Governance

The other key feature of pre-agrarian society is its self-governance. Managing food security is decentralized to informal consumption communities and is independent of state regulation or policy. The only extent to which the state gets involved is as a resource that can be tapped especially in the case of emergency. The more common pattern, however, is that persons from member households who have moved away from their rural location retain status in the community by remitting financial support to ensure that nobody goes hungry. The fact that international remittances by Africans in the diaspora to their brethren back home exceed the amount of money that the international donor community disburses every year is testimony to the continued strength of the moral imperatives of such a society. According to the World Bank (2019), the total amount going to sub-Saharan Africa in 2018 was US$46 billion, which was lower than remittances to other regions, yet at a level close to the disbursement by the international OECD donor community. The latter, according to the World Bank, that same year was US$50 billion. The continued strength of pre-agrarian norms and values throughout Africa means that they retain not only an unusual degree of autonomy but also strength to withstand state pressure by falling back on self-governance. As I noted over forty years ago, the African peasantry, in comparison with its counterpart in agrarian societies, is largely uncaptured by the state (Hyden 1980) and has remained so to this day.

### 3.4   CONSEQUENCES FOR POLITICS

This disconnect between state and society means that African politics is not easy to subsume in theoretical frames constructed on the empirical evidence of social formations in other regions of the world. Three features stand out: (1) the weakness of voluntary action, (2) the absence of ideology, and (3) the strength of external actors. Each of these deserves elaboration here.

### 3.4.1   *Weakness of Voluntary Action*

Africa is the home of community-based organizations (CBOs). These associations are the dominant form of social organization beyond the primary family and kinship structures. CBOs are not voluntary in the way the Red Cross Society or Save the Children are although they serve the same purpose of securing the welfare of people in need. Voluntary organizations are formed by people who want to help others. The purpose of community organizations, in contrast, is to help members. There is no rationale for campaigning to help others, nor is there reason for organizing to influence the state. The foundation for the type of civic life that characterizes Western society is missing.

Theorizing in Comparative Politics usually presupposes such a foundation for voluntary action, and it is generally regarded as an integral part of the development of democratic governance. This associational life is the product of modern society that has already been differentiated by such forces as mature capitalism, industrialization, and urbanization. In Africa, these forces have yet to reshape society. To the extent that associational life exists at all, civil society organizations are present in the national capital, but they are generally weak, the main reason being that support of the community pre-empts support of voluntary causes linked to the public good. The rise of an African middle class may change this, but for now the closest African societies come to supporting voluntary action is through faith-based organizations. They are important when it comes to organizing social life but rarely engage in politics.

The weakness of the voluntary sector also means that there is no real social contract in African society. Community organizations see no systemic need for the state (Hyden 1980). This orientation in African society is reinforced by the colonial origin of the state. The legitimacy of "public institutions" in Africa rests on how far they "leak" resources to rivalling communities anxious to boost their welfare. Accessing these public funds is best done by relying on a well-placed and influential intermediary – patron – who can engage in transactions with public servants to switch the use of official resources in his favour. Patrons represent communities of consumption, most of which in African politics are ethnic in character. It is taken for granted that these intermediaries have the right to take a "commission" for their effort. Patrons get away with enriching themselves as long as it is not perceived as excessive or harmful to the community. Such is the way that state–society relations in African countries tend to be structured and managed. These relations give rise to what Bayart (1993) calls the "politics of the belly" and North et al. (2009) describe as the "natural state" characterized by informality and elite control of access. It is also the reason why elections in Africa tend to be about the "right to eat", that is, having access to government power and the control of public funds that follows (Lindberg 2003; Wrong 2009). Corruption, therefore, is hardly just a mark of deviant behaviour. It is a practice that grows out of the structural realities of African society much like it did in other regions before their modernization rendered "limited access" regimes less useful for national development. Even if corruption has continued in modern society, the institutional mechanisms for curbing it have been strengthened to the point where corruption today is viewed as deviant and subject to public condemnation.

## 3.4.2 *Absence of Ideology*

Social formations in Africa also have the effect of lessening the need for a form of politics based on ideology or systematized positions on public policy. Because these formations are based on communities that share the same interest in having access to public resources to boost their own welfare, political competition does not reflect opposite economic interests as the case is in modern society. In the latter, whether conservative or radical, these views of society share a forward-looking perspective based on how the "national cake" can be made greater and more productive. This has not changed with the creation of "green" parties focused on resource conservation. In fact, as their influence has increased, the concern about future resource use has become an even more pronounced part of public discourse in modern society. It has added a new dimension to the ideological landscape, but it has not changed the significance that ideology plays in modern society.

Perhaps the most important role that ideology typically plays in politics is to offer the perspective in which policy is debated and formulated. Without being linked to policy, ideology loses much of its rationale. This interpretation, which is taken for granted in comparative politics theory, is largely lacking in contemporary African politics. Ideology played a significant role during the short period of decolonization, especially in urban working-class circles (Cooper 1996). Once in power, however, the nationalist leaders engaged in measures to limit the influence of modernizing forces outside government, both capitalists and workers. To the extent that there is a local ideological content in African politics today, it tends to centre on how governance should be organized – for example, centrally, federally, or in the form of devolution. Otherwise, it is present only in policy statements such as Vision 2030 or national sustainable development strategies that are required as part of the country's participation in internationally driven policy agreements. As Markovitz (1969) already noted many years ago, these accords are typically more symbolic than material.

### 3.4.3  Strength of External Actors

Africa's endogenous social formations have proved to be resilient and sufficiently adaptable to make a difference to this day. They withstood the onslaught by the colonial powers to modernize society in their own image. Prevailing social formations are still not really captured by the state. Instead, they produce an alternative informal arrangement, what I have labelled the "economy of affection" (Hyden 1980). Most notably, the rational-legal character of the inherited state bureaucracy was subverted in favour of political expediency (Rweyemamu and Hyden 1975). The result is that since independence the African state has become more "natural" in the sense of being driven by sectional interests in society rather than emerging as a centre of power capable of shaping society in its own image. It is not a driver of change as is typically assumed in the literature on the state (Skocpol 1979; Migdal 1988).

It is this shortcoming that has left so much political space to foreign actors on the African political scene. The prevalence of foreign aid has been good for Africa in many respects, notably the expansion of the education and health sectors while foreign investments have allowed the development of both infrastructure and manufacturing. It is the aid agencies and foreign investors, however, who have become the real drivers of change in many countries of the region. Their policy conditions and demand for effective use of the aid set the parameters for what the state in Africa is typically doing. With the bulk of the development budget and much of the recurrent budget being funded by outside sources, the African state is more an intermediary than a true change agent (see, e.g., Sundberg 2019).

Most external input has been focused on strengthening the state and its policy programmes, but especially in the past two decades, external funds have also been channelled to boost the influence of society-based organizations. A range of international non-governmental organizations committed to the global Agenda 2030 with its sustainable development goals have become the most vocal advocates of a coherent policy agenda. This agenda, however, is not always locally anchored and tends to pre-empt the role of domestic organizations (Mercer 2002). It may address issues of poverty reduction, but an equally significant preoccupation of these international organizations has been to "coach" local counterpart organizations and turn them into clones of themselves. This exercise is politically controversial in many of the countries because governments perceive the international non-governmental organizations as carriers of "foreign values" (Manji and O'Coill 2002).

## 3.5   CONCLUSIONS

Although it is generally acknowledged that politics reflects its social base, during the last three decades, the research frontier in Comparative Politics has lied elsewhere, notably in the study of institutions and more specifically democracy. The limits of this research orientation have become evident with the backlash that democracy has suffered across the world. The reasons why this reversal has occurred need to be examined beyond a narrow focus on the demise of democratic institutions. It has underlying causes, and these differ from region to region of the world and in Africa frequently from country to country. This chapter has drawn attention to the specificity of the social formations in the African region and how they contribute to making politics quite different from the assumptions made in much of Comparative Politics theorizing, whether it focuses on institutions or democracy at large. By highlighting how social formations in Africa have evolved along a different trajectory compared with elsewhere in the world, it has shown how the very basis of politics in Africa makes its integration into institution-based analysis an unenviable challenge. The colonial powers tried to reshape African society in their own image but the African resistance to this enterprise aborted this process prematurely. The disconnect between state and society remains and needs further elaboration, initially by examining the role of the state in countries where a true national community is yet to be formed and an effective system of governance that links citizens to their state is at best at an incipient stage.

# 4 Nation-States and State-Nations

INTRODUCTION

The state concept is one of the oldest in the study of politics. It features prominently in the analyses of the founders of modern social science, Max Weber and Karl Marx, the former focusing especially on its inner workings, that is, the state as organization, the latter on its relation to society. Marx had a critical perspective on the state, viewing it as an instrument of exploitation in the hands of those controlling capital. Even though he differed from Marx, Joseph Schumpeter (1942) later elaborated on the role of capitalism in social transformation, arguing that it is a process of "creative destruction". Even if it carries its own costs, it is historically necessary.

Since these early days in social science research on the state, its position in Comparative Politics has been one of on and off, initially relating to its role in economic development but later, following the rise of African countries to independent statehood, also to the issue of nation-building. The result is the emergence of two research traditions, one centred on statecraft, the other on statehood. Although they are related, they have ended up in different fields of the discipline, the former in Comparative Politics (and to some extent Public Policy and Administration), the latter in International Relations. Research on statecraft – or governance as it has also been called in recent years – produced a rich literature on the welfare state (e.g., Rimlinger 1971; Esping-Andersen 1985; Katzenstein 1985) and a complementary track devoted to corporatism (e.g., Lehmbruch and Schmitter 1982; Huber and Stephens 2001; Steinmo 2010). Much of this coincided with the call to "bring the state back in" (Evans et al. 1985) in an edited volume that was reprinted several times in the ensuing years. This upsurge in research on the state was very much in reaction to the growing influence of the rational (or public) choice literature that had been imported from economics. The importance of this literature on the state was that it covered other regions than Europe. By focusing on Asia as well as Latin America, new perspectives developed, notably the concept of the "developmental state" drawn from the East Asian experience (Johnson 1982; Woh-Cumings 2001; Low 2004).

Much of the state literature has assumed the presence of an already cohesive political community, the nation-state. State formation in Europe and Asia was the outcome of the dissolution of empires. The emerging states in the early twentieth century were all grounded in specific national groups. Despite immigration to Europe in recent decades, the dominance of the original national community has continued. Integration of the newcomers, therefore, has become a prominent political issue in these countries (Stepan et al. 2011).

African states were also born out of the end of empire, but they were not formed around nationalities. The colonial powers had assembled a range of pre-agrarian societies into territories with the purpose of conquest and development. Thus, as Africans struggled to gain independence, they had to accept a statehood that was not aligned to nationhood. There were a few exceptions such as Eswatini, Lesotho, and Rwanda but most of the new states in Africa faced the unfinished task of nation-building. African leaders themselves decided at an Organization of African Unity meeting in Addis Ababa in December 1963 that the colonial borders should remain intact. These leaders, therefore, did not take over nation-states but accepted to govern state-nations, that is, countries where loyalty to the state takes on greater significance than the individual rights of citizens (Joseph 1999).

## 4.2   THE RISE OF THE NATION-STATE

Even though research on the nation-state includes multiple regions of the world, the leading edge is related to its emergence in European context. Studies of the formation of statehood in the late nineteenth century have often served as benchmark for subsequent research on the subject. Two things are important about the role of the European experience in research on the state. The first is that statehood occurred at a time of great social transformation through industrialization, urbanization, and new forms of social and economic inequality arising from the growth of capitalism. The second thing is that state formation was driven by already existing nationalities, all of them agitating for political sovereignty. This is how the concept of nation-state took hold in comparative analysis. It refers to a state that derives its legitimacy largely from serving a group of people who share the determinants of a common culture, notably language, and can relate to a shared historical experience. In Europe, the nation-state was the result of battles between nationalities to gain control of their own destiny, a principle that obtained international legitimacy through the 1919 Peace Treaty in Versailles at the end of the First World War. The number of states in the world quickly shot up as empires were broken up and independent countries were created around nationalities. President Woodrow Wilson – the most influential world leader at Versailles – argued in his famous "Fourteen Points" speech that each peace-loving nation should have the right to live its own life, determine its own institutions, be assured of justice, and a fair dealing by the other peoples of the world. More specifically, this led to the restoration of Belgium as a sovereign state, the creation of an independent Polish state, the cessation of occupation of Romania, Serbia, and Montenegro, and security guarantees for the Turkish portions of the defeated Ottoman Empire. Furthermore, Wilson argued that territory should be allocated with respect to the composition of its residents. For example, like the new nation-state of Poland, the borders of Italy should be defined along clearly recognizable lines of nationality (Tilly 1975). The president's speech was primarily for a European audience. He did refer to anti-colonial claims along the same lines as European nationalities, but the Versailles Conference never discussed what the Wilsonian principles would mean for Nigerians, Kenyans, or Angolans. Instead, discussions regarding Africa were about who would take responsibility for the colonies surrendered by the defeated Germany.

The Wilsonian principles of national sovereignty, however, did not die and were reasserted by Africans as they formulated their claims for self-determination a generation later. The decolonization process after the Second World War, therefore, set in motion another process of reorganizing the political map of the world. This time it became difficult to apply the principle of self-determination based on nationality. Among the many colonies that sought independence there were few self-evident claims based on a shared national heritage. Instead of putting nationality first, the African decolonization process was launched on the opposite principle – that the state must forge a nation. The territorial entities, which had been politically and administratively organized by the colonial powers, became the foundation on which national sovereignty in Africa would be based. It fell upon the leaders of these newly independent state entities to bring together people who were used to identify primarily with their own ethnic group. This was no easy task. The experience of being under the colonial yoke was the most important thing that these ethnic groups shared as they moved towards political independence. The language of the colonial masters was typically spoken only by a small elite. Sorting out how to deal with multiple ethnicities within a single state made the process different from what occurred in Europe a generation earlier. Instead of forming nation-states, African countries were faced with the task of building state-nations.

Africa has the largest number of state-nations in the world, but the concept has hardly ever been used in comparative research since Crawford Young (1976), as noted in Chapter 2, introduced it in his comparison of ex-colonial states in Asia and Africa. As a more recent account of "crafting the state-nation" (Stepan et al. 2011) suggests, the concept has been used primarily to examine how existing nation-states cope with multi-culturalism. The focus has been on how immigration of new minorities leads to greater cultural heterogeneity and the emergence of a politics of identity. This happens in the European Union where, in addition to internal migration from poorer to richer member countries, there has been an influx of bona fide refugees as well as economic migrants from the Middle East and Africa. In the contemporary global context, therefore, the state-nation concept is likely to take on greater salience in Comparative Politics research.

This chapter extends the use of this concept to the African governance scene and examines the specific challenges that stem from the dual threat of a state that is not an organic outgrowth of society and a population that is divided by ethnicity or religion. African political leaders routinely face this double wham, and it tends to be their prime governance preoccupation. It is in this context that they must also consider bringing in a liberal form of democracy. Balancing these rivalling concerns is not an easy exercise and, as will be discussed further in Chapters 5 and 8, African government leaders have adopted different strategies in building a cohesive national political community.

## 4.3   THE STATE-NATION CONCEPT

A state-nation is a political system that manages diversity while also striving to build a sense of belonging with respect to the larger political community (Stepan et al. 2011). It recognizes both the centripetal and centrifugal nature of politics in societies that are characterized by ethnic diversity, often geographically concentrated. Examples of state-nations in the West would be countries like Canada, Belgium, and Spain and in the developing regions, India, Pakistan, Philippines, and Indonesia. They are contrasted with countries like Japan, Thailand, Germany, France, and the Scandinavian countries that have more organically over time grown into nation-states. France, for example, was for many centuries inhabited by groups of people with their own language and culture, but since the days of Napoleon and his policy of homogenizing the country, France has gradually become a country speaking one language and people viewing themselves proudly as French. Eugen Weber (1976) has shown how the French central state,

Table 4.1 *Comparison of nation-state and state-nation*

| Variable | Nation-state | State-nation |
|---|---|---|
| Pre-existing condition | Awareness of and attachment to one dominant cultural tradition | Awareness of and attachment to more than one cultural tradition |
| Development scenario | Organic homogenization | Manufactured integration of consensus |
| Dominant form of politics | Competition between interest-based parties and organizations | Rivalry over state power among identity-based groups |
| State policy | Assimilation of new groups | Creation of a sense of belonging to the political community at large |
| Citizen orientation | Acceptance of a single national identity | Presence of multiple cross-cutting identities |

*Source:* Author

using military conscription and compulsory public schooling, turned Catalans, Corsicans, Gascons, Normans, Picards, Vendéens, Basques, Bretons, and a host of others into Frenchmen. The diversities that once so deeply defined the population were flattened. The differences between nation-state and state-nation are summarized in Table 4.1.

The dilemma of many state-nations, especially in the global South, is that they must be capable of accelerating development while simultaneously crafting a national political community. These two ambitions often collide, leading to conflict instigated, as Boone (2014) shows, over property regime. Development entails privatizing land tenure, a policy that calls for a turnover of deeply rooted principles of communal ownership. Even though much of this risk is being managed within consumption communities at the local level, it easily becomes a political issue when privatization is driven by outsiders with a profit motive and with no previous connection to the local area. Such circumstances may pose threats to national unity and social stability. For local communities, there is no such a

thing as empty land. Whether in fallow or not in use for other reasons, land today always historically belongs to one community or
another. Outsiders seeing large stretches of land not being used view
this as an investment opportunity. It is such opportunities that have
brought not only multi-national corporations to develop land in the
more scarcely populated countries in the region but also Chinese
immigrants for whom any uncultivated land is viewed as a waste.
Like European farmers before, many have settled in Africa culti-
vating the land with African partners to mitigate the conflict over
ownership that their presence causes (Alden 2013). The long-term
lease that these Chinese settlers are seeking – and often given by
government – is a potential source of friction.

## 4.4  THE AFRICAN STATE-NATION

The state in pre-agrarian society is not territorial. Its hegemony
rests on control over people, not land. Its monopoly of exercising
force, therefore, is more social and cultural than physical and legal.
Power is not exercised in a systemic manner. Instead, it stems from
discretionary control of access to scarce resources, whether material or social, much like North et al. (2009) describe the "natural
state". Its power is soft and is exercised through means such as co-
optation and mutual transactions. Why, then, do African countries
rank as some of the most conflict-ridden places in the world, as confirmed by, for example, Bakken and Rustad (2018), who show that
state-based conflicts (i.e., conflicts where the state is at least one
of the actors) have continued to be a significant part of the political landscape in Africa in the first two decades of the new century?
For example, according to the same source, there were as many as
eighteen of them in 2017.

   The answer to why so many African countries are conflict-
ridden is the weak alignment between state and nation and their
exposure to external forces. Governance is not just the management of public affairs within an already institutionalized hierarchy
of authority as the case tends to be in nation-states. The state that

Africans inherited from the colonial powers was not like any other state, although it was modelled on the modern state of the metropolitan countries. Because it was a late construction compared to the colonial states established in Asia and Latin America, its origin in the late nineteenth century coincided with the spread of capitalism and the urge for modernization. Linked as it was to the metropole, it was an externally enforced institution that lacked legitimacy because of the coercive way it presented itself to African society. This thesis is most thoroughly argued by Young (1994) in his comparative discussion of the African colonial state. It signified a much more brutal break with the past than similar colonial projects did in other developing regions. To a large extent because there was not enough revenue to finance it, the colonial state in Africa had to rely on force and the use of its security arm. In the Belgian Congo where the state was especially brutal, Africans used the expression *Bula Matari* – the crusher of rocks – to refer to the colonial state. While there is little doubt that colonization caused a lot of pain in African society, it never fully erased the legacy of pre-colonial structures, some of which, as noted in Chapter 2, were mature chiefdoms, others acephalous (stateless) societies. The continuation of multiple chiefdoms within a single national territory has posed an especially grave challenge to managing the African state-nation in the post-independence period. It has been a prominent subject of analysis in Africanist research (e.g., Crowder and Ikime 1970; Lemarchand 1977; Skalník 1999).

Mamdani (1996) coined the concept of "the bifurcated state" referring to the rivalry that developed after independence between a national "civic" authority and another type of authority at the sub-national level drawing its legitimacy from a pre-agrarian society legacy. Using Uganda as the prime illustration he showed how the system of "indirect rule" that the British practised in the country brought civic consciousness to the urban population but left those in the countryside as subjects at the whim of autocratic local chiefs. He further argues that although the French in theory used a system of direct rule, that is, insisting on the qualification of "Frenchhood" as a condition for public employment, their governance practice left a legacy reminiscent of that of the British. His point is that this legacy across Africa – the bifurcation of political authority at the national and sub-national levels – is a principal reason why countries have proved unstable and find democratization a tough challenge. Ndegwa (1997) has addressed the same issue demonstrating the tension between citizenship and ethnicity in Kenya, and more recently Arreola (2013) has examined it through his research on protesting and policing in multi-ethnic authoritarian states.

Catherine Boone (2014), who has examined the relationship between property rights and political authority in different African countries, discusses the issues that arise as the political elite tries to anchor the state in a pre-agrarian society undergoing change. Her analysis highlights the challenges associated with the transition to agrarian society in which the state tries to set and sustain an order created in its own image. Her account of the various cases of land conflict can also be read as the ambition of an incipient middle class to cement national coherence based on a liberal property regime rather than the legacy of variable communal property systems.

The state in Africa, therefore, is involved in a constant political struggle to establish itself as the institution with monopoly to use force. In other regions of the world, this is not such a prominent issue because there is greater congruence between state policy and the capacity to implement it. The African state is weak, as Herbst (2000) argues, in the sense that preoccupation with statehood tends to limit its ability to engage in successful statecraft through an independent bureaucracy (Levi 1989). This is evident not the least in the Sahel region, where ironically the trade routes across the Sahara Desert that were so important for the rise of its kingdoms have now, not the least because of the political collapse of Libya, become passageways for terrorists aiming to delegitimize and destroy the local state structures in place.

## 4.5   THE "GOVERNMENTALITY" WEAKNESS

The African state-nation is still a project in the making. The politics of forging the nation and subjecting society to schemes, ideologies, and systems that make it possible for the state to realize its objectives is still the prime governance challenge. In mature nation-states, individuals typically manage themselves in ways that agree with the state's notion of good conduct. That is much less so in African countries, where "governmentality", Foucault's concept (Gordon 1991), is still an issue because people are not yet organized according to shared economic interest but rather in communities with their own culture. Because African leaders must balance the conflicting pressures from their tribe and the larger political community, the ensuing political discourse does not enforce the development of the instruments the state needs to conduct its business. Instead, it encourages modes of governance that are either rivalrous or monopolistic. Any lasting political settlement is a transactional compromise involving power-sharing rather than an institutional arrangement to facilitate the conduct of state business. Success in the pursuit of such a compact often involves the use of informal institutions that help overcome the rigidity of formal rules. For example, in Tanzania with its 120 different ethnic groups, some large but many small, political practice inside the ruling party – Tanganyika African National Union, later renamed Chama cha Mapinduzi (Revolutionary Party) – has evolved whereby the presidential candidate is nominated from a small ethnic group to reduce the risk of tribalist sentiments emerging as a threat to national unity. Similar informal rules have developed in other African countries to facilitate transactional forms of governance. One especially common such rule is to ensure the appointment of cabinet members that are reflective of the country's ethnic and religious composition. This approach to managing national coherence is largely based on unofficial transactional agreements that are quite different from those made in a system of the rule of law.

Because of the prevalence of informal social exchanges, the state encounters limitations in how far the economy can be controlled.

Practices outside the formal law such as tax evasion are common and therefore a source of frustration for conscientious policy-makers. Neither the carrot of a rational strategy based on a recognized development ideology nor the stick of a well-organized and trained security force has proved powerful enough to reduce the impact of the informal means of managing the affairs of the state-nation. This informality raises the issue of the state's effectiveness as a driver of change. Transactional politics does not necessarily strengthen national unity because it requires no absolute submission to the values of the wider national political community (Joseph 1987; Obadare and Ebenezer 2013). Dual identities are common in African countries and managing them comes with definite costs, both economic and political. In addition to the challenges of keeping statehood intact, the transactional nature of politics in African countries poses a threat to the development of the institutional requirements of statecraft. Because the population is not fully captured by the state, when it tries to intervene, it typically does so in an arbitrary manner that causes resistance rather than compliance.

The difficulties of crafting the state-nation are reflected in international measures of government effectiveness. The World Governance Indicators showed that compared to other regions of the world, on an aggregate basis, sub-Saharan Africa demonstrated the lowest level of effectiveness in 2018 (World Bank 2019). A vast majority of African states fell below the medium score, indicating the absence of effective governance institutions to link government and citizenry. Only six countries – Botswana, Cap Verde, Namibia, Seychelles, South Africa, and Rwanda – scored above the median. The first five of them have not had issues relating to statehood. As a result, they have been able to concentrate on accelerating national development and reaching a level that makes them among the most developed on the continent. Rwanda has been able to do so by reinventing institutions dating back to its pre-colonial kingdom. This constitutional arrangement amounts to a form of participatory democracy where the principal government objective is to pre-empt

or punish dissent. A polity with similar features has been put in place
by President Yoweri Museveni in neighbouring Uganda (Green 2011).

## 4.6   CONCLUSIONS

The concept of state-nation has become more widely applicable in
recent years as many states, not the least in Europe, are getting more
heterogenous and thus need to be governed with more attention to
managing multiple identities. This means that the state is being polit-
icized in new ways that citizens in these countries have not experienced before. Although Stepan et al. (2011) use India as the prime
example, it may be the African experience with the state-nation that
is the most relevant and informative case. As the account in this
chapter has suggested, it provides theoretical insights that apply to
other regions, notably the importance of informal institutions and
how state imperatives shape regime structures. Even though Africa
does not always get the scholarly attention that it deserves, it does
provide insights that are both theoretically and politically applicable
more widely as globalization and the presence of greater geographical
mobility affect statehood and statecraft in ways that make nation-
states and state-nations increasingly similar. This scenario obviously
has implications for how we study not only the state but also other
institutions in politics.

# 5    Regimes and Institutions

The regime concept has featured prominently in Comparative Politics in the last three decades. In the comparative democratization literature, the notion of regime transition and consolidation has provided the direction of much research across regions of the world. It has generated interest in measuring the progress countries make in becoming democratic systems. The indicators provided by Freedom House and the more recently established Varieties of Democracy Institute constitute valuable data for these global comparisons. The merit of relying primarily on such indicators, however, has increasingly come into question as political developments around the world challenge the notion that democracy is the only type of regime that matters. The significant backsliding in recent years confirms the rise of new challenges to democracy (Bermeo 2016; Waldner and Lust 2018). Parallel with this reversal, countries around the world are developing their own regimes reflecting the social and economic conditions on the ground. These structural factors explain, among other things, the rise of populist leaders who may allow electoral competition but put restrictions on other democratic rights (Levitsky and Way 2010). These leaders are a product of changes in society, not just examples of deviant political behaviour.

More recently, some comparativists, such as Lührmann and Lindberg (2019), have suggested that referring to non-democratic regimes as hybrid is misleading because there is clearly a strong wave of autocratization already going on at present. Basing themselves on the Varieties of Democracy data, they suggest, however, that we should not worry because in a comparative historical perspective it is not as threatening as previous such waves. The problem with this interpretation is that crunching numbers alone provides a sketchy analysis of what is happening. Their concluding advice, therefore, for more research is welcome. The emerging autocratic regimes do not necessarily follow the same dynamic process. It is too simple to assume that leaders have "got tired" of democracy or citizens are no longer as committed as they were when the democratization wave began in the 1990s. Democracy (or autocracy) does not operate in a socio-economic vacuum. How political systems work is very much a reflection of changes in the underlying political economy, both domestic and international. As scientists we have an obligation to problematize democracy in its wider contemporary social and political setting.

Two issues are of special interest in highlighting how regime studies in Africa may contribute to rejuvenating comparative political studies at a time when a sole focus on the levels of democracy is losing its edge. The first is how we study regime change, the second how we understand and handle the concept of institution. Democratization research has so far focused on a preconceived model of democracy and adjusted the analysis accordingly. It has been all about degree of adoption and compliance rather than a search for how regimes come about. The latter, though, is key to understanding the variable paths that countries take in their political development. Regimes are not necessarily institutional arrangements, fixed once and for all. In Africa's state-nations, for example, this is evident in the continued prevalence of informal formulas of conducting politics. The scope of Comparative Politics studies, therefore, should be widened to incorporate issues arising from regime formation in uncertain conditions, a call made already many years ago by Schaffer (1998). The purpose of this chapter is to bring back a focus on regime formation with prime reference to the Africa region.

## 5.2    DEMOCRATIZATION WITHOUT WAVES

When democratization began in Latin America in the 1980s and a parallel move took place in Eastern Europe, Huntington (1991) set the tone for comparative studies by describing these events as amounting to a "third wave of democratization". His image of what was happening around the world was reinforced by Fukuyama (1992), who argued that, with countries everywhere having turned to liberal democracy, our world has reached the "end of history" as we have known it. The third wave made a difference in regions like Latin America and Eastern Europe (O'Donnell and Schmitter 1986; Whitehead 2001; Mainwaring and Hagopian 2005). Citizens celebrated when new leaders embraced civil and political rights for all and brought back competitive elections for government office. Whether this involved saying goodbye to military or communist rule, it was a historical event – a critical juncture for politics in both regions.

Democratization in Africa began in a less dramatic fashion. As Bratton and van de Walle (1997) show in their analysis, protests started in some countries but not in others. What occurred in one country got little publicity in others, including those close by. Government leaders did not want information about these events to spread and the media were typically cowed into silence. This "bubbling-up-here-and-there" was not insignificant, but these instances never turned into social movements or a real region-wide wave. These protests were what Bleck and van de Walle (2012) and Harris and Hearn (2018) subsequently labelled "valence" protests, that is, ways of expressing voice between elections without the requirements of a formal social or political organization. What helped make these protests turn into a continent-wide process of democratization was the support given by Western donors. Where governments did not accept the coming of a new order, donors strived to strengthen civil society organizations – some genuine, others fake. This support has no doubt helped civil society organizations to become a voice in governance, but the argument has also been made that it might have tempered activism and the capacity of these organizations to serve as drivers of change (Hearn 2000). Receiving money from Western donors comes with a potential political cost for Africa's civil society actors. As civil society has grown in strength in many countries, this point may be less applicable today but organizing collective action for democratic causes in a sustainable manner remains a challenge in societies divided along ethnic or racial lines. Shifting social cleavages from these lines and reordering society along class lines is at best a process in its beginning stage. Protest waves in African countries during 2011–16 notwithstanding (Mueller 2018), social class consciousness is hardly the driver of democratic development that it was in Europe a century ago. Overthrowing autocracy is one thing, building democracy another. Protest is only a first step and not itself evidence of democratic transition. Without a historical perspective on institutions, it is easy to overdramatize the impact of single current events. Democratization in African countries may have benefitted from the tailwind that the wave provided across the world, but it has also encountered obstacles – not in the form of explicit right-wing or fascist opposition but in the form of the absence of strong domestic social forces to drive the project.

This becomes evident in a closer examination of democratization at the sub-regional level (Table 5.1). Although West and Southern Africa score higher on the Varieties of Democracy Index than countries in the East and Central sub-regions, each has both good and poor performers. The only true crystallization of democratic values can be found in Southern Africa where Botswana, Namibia, and South Africa constitute a democratic core very much attributable to the region's relatively high economic development and the presence of more pronounced social class cleavages. Another notable feature of the African democracy scene is how the small island states in the Atlantic and Indian Oceans tend to outperform states on the African mainland. Mauritius and the Seychelles to the east and Cape Verde and Sao Tomé e Principe to the west are among the high scorers (but the larger island nation of Madagascar does not fall in this category). For the island states, both location and size make a difference.

Because democratization in Africa, as Bratton and van de Walle (1997) demonstrate, has resulted from the burst of local protest events rather than a transformative wave, there is no single model for how to sustain a transition to democracy. For example, in the absence of

Table 5.1 *Level of democracy in Africa by sub-region*

| Sub-region/country | Score | Sub-region/country | Score |
|---|---|---|---|
| *West Africa* (16) | | *East Africa* (12) | |
| Cape Verde | 0.715 | Seychelles | 0.452 |
| Benin | 0.612 | Tanzania | 0.386 |
| Senegal | 0.577 | Kenya | 0.333 |
| Ghana | 0.537 | Uganda | 0.279 |
| Burkina Faso | 0.503 | Rwanda | 0.205 |
| Liberia | 0.490 | Somalia | 0.138 |
| Nigeria | 0.451 | Djibouti | 0.126 |
| Mali | 0.393 | Ethiopia | 0.107 |
| Niger | 0.376 | Sudan | 0.106 |
| Sierra Leone | 0.372 | South Sudan | 0.058 |
| Côte d'Ivoire | 0.369 | Burundi | 0.055 |
| Guinea-Bissau | 0.316 | Eritrea | 0.016 |
| Gambia | 0.296 | **Average** | **0.199** |
| Togo | 0.240 | | |
| Guinea | 0.214 | *Southern Africa* (13) | |
| Mauritania | 0.158 | Mauritius | 0.696 |
| **Average** | **0.409** | South Africa | 0.622 |
| | | Namibia | 0.578 |
| *Central Africa* (8) | | Botswana | 0.576 |
| São Tomé and Principe | 0.607 | Malawi | 0.474 |
| Gabon | 0.289 | Lesotho | 0.424 |
| Central African Republic | 0.232 | Mozambique | 0.327 |
| Cameroon | 0.154 | Zambia | 0.276 |
| Congo Republic | 0.110 | Madagascar | 0.263 |
| Democratic Rep. of Congo | 0.104 | Comoros | 0.252 |
| Chad | 0.094 | Zimbabwe | 0.200 |
| Equatorial Guinea | 0.053 | Angola | 0.141 |
| **Average** | **0.205** | Swaziland | 0.100 |
| | | **Average** | **0.398** |

Legend: 0 = low; 1 = high
*Source:* Varieties of Democracy Annual Report (2019)

success stories in the region, Botswana was for a long time considered an exemplary case of democracy. As a presumed model, however, it failed to inspire leaders from other countries. In the African context, there has been no equivalent to Brazil or Poland to serve as a beacon for the whole region. Democracy has lacked the contagion effect that it had in Latin America, Eastern Europe, and – to a lesser extent – in the Middle East and North Africa region during the Arab Spring.

Africa has also lacked a robust regional mechanism for monitoring and enforcing democratic values. There has been no equivalent to the Council of Europe or the Organization of American States to keep tab on political developments in member countries. The African Union has been primarily concerned with continent-wide security issues and has deliberately avoided getting involved in the domestic affairs of individual countries. To the extent that any monitoring of democracy takes place, it is bodies at the sub-regional level that have tried to respond. A prime example is the sub-regional body for West Africa – the Economic Community of West African States – that has been actively intervening not only to stop the civil wars in Liberia and Sierra Leone but also to prevent member countries from turning to outright autocracy. The Southern Africa Development Community has also been active in monitoring member states and in the case of the attempted coup in Lesotho in 2014 intervened to save its democratic system. Equivalent bodies in Central and East Africa have been more hesitant to intervene in the affairs of their member countries. For example, in 2015 the leaders of the East African Community failed to intervene in Burundi to stop the then president, Pierre Nkurunziza, from changing the country's constitution to be able to continue in power beyond the stipulated two terms in office.[1] The sub-region lacks a leading country like South Africa in the South and Nigeria in the West. Furthermore, the other East African leaders with their autocratic record of rule are accused of lacking the moral authority for a credible intervention in another country's internal affairs. This is another reminder that the principles of democracy are secondary to national sovereignty and unity.

---

[1] Nkurunziza died from cardiac arrest in June 2020, only a short time after he had completed his third term and had stepped down from office.

## 5.3   REGIMES STILL IN THE MAKING

Successful regimes are not built over night. The emergence as well as acceptance of democratic constitutions and accompanying systems of the rule of law in Europe was sequenced over several generations. It was a step-by-step maturing process. The result is that Europe's democratic regimes today rest on a solid foundation. Opposition to democracy occurs but in a comparative perspective these regimes have a degree of solidity that reduces the risk that backsliding ends in regime collapse.

The situation in Africa's state-nations is different. Ever since independence, African countries have struggled to stabilize norms into lasting constitutions (Prempeh 2007). Instead of enjoying the bonus of sequencing, as in Europe (and other regions albeit in different circumstances), African countries, under pressure from both domestic and international sources, have been forced to implement reforms in a much shorter timeframe (Meyerrose 2020). The fact that the African countries inherited the state from their colonial masters exacerbates the difficulties of finding the right blend of norms for constitutional reforms. Where nationhood must be manufactured out of pre-agrarian conditions, the prime issue is how to reconcile rivalry among communities for whom the concept of a nation is not only new but often also foreign. The story emerging from the rise of democratic regimes in Western Europe is quite homogenous, but that is not the case with post-independence developments in Africa. They have been remarkably varied. Donor pressure notwithstanding, regimes have evolved largely in response to local conditions. Two factors have been especially important in determining regime formation since independence: the degree of political stability and political inclusiveness. How good have they been in pre-empting conflict, how good at directing an inclusive form of politics?

Conflicts and breakdowns have played their part in several countries since independence, but many others have enjoyed a largely peaceful state-nation development. For regime purposes, therefore, countries can be divided into those with a stable political path and those with a largely unstable course characterized by government overthrows often leading to civil war. The first group of states tends to have lasting political settlements but can still be distinguished in terms of how plural or monolithic their system of governance is. For example, one distinct pattern is those countries that gained independence through an influential nationalist or liberation movement. Tanzania and several countries in southern Africa are cases in point. Here power is centralized and monolithic through the extensive control of the state by a movement party. In many other countries enjoying continuity of peace and a lasting political settlement, governance has emerged as plural, clientelist, and competitive, sometimes to the point of rocking the very order itself. Kenya and Senegal are examples of such plural, clientelist, and competitive governance where the challenge has been to constitutionalize pluralism in ways that overcome the prevailing ethnic and religious cleavages.

The second group is likewise divided by two tendencies. One is a clear break with the past and the evolution of a new order based on the commitment of a dominant ruling party or state to guarantee peace and accelerate development. Rwanda and Ethiopia are examples of this authoritarian-modernizing tendency. Countries belonging to this category may vary in their emphasis on control and modernization, but they all have in common the belief that development is more important than democracy (Grundy 1996). The other tendency is typical of countries that are so deeply fractured that governance requires a flexible coalitional approach. Because these coalitions rarely hold together, authority tends to end up in the hands of a "strongman" using both co-optation and intimidation to keep the country together. Uganda, which has one of the most complex cleavage patterns in Africa, is a case in point. While the National Resistance Movement initially was a true movement structure, sustaining it in the context of the country's strong indigenous structures has proved a frustrating exercise for the country's president, Yoweri Museveni, who led the rise to power of the National Resistance

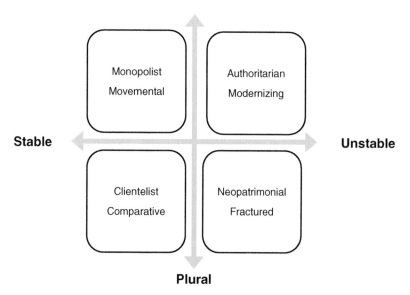

**Inclusivist**

| Monopolist Movemental | Authoritarian Modernizing |
| Clientelist Comparative | Neopatrimonial Fractured |

**Stable** ← → **Unstable**

**Plural**

FIGURE 5.1 Predominant types of regimes in Africa
Source: Author

Movement. It has since disintegrated, and governance in Uganda is more appropriately labelled "neo-patrimonial and fractured" because it relies on placating and integrating powerful kingdoms in the south and acephalous (stateless) communities in the north into a single nation capable of also modernizing (Tripp 2010). It is no coincidence that Uganda is one of the most conservative countries in Africa because the cultural influence of its powerful pre-colonial states is still very much part of the country's approach to modernization. The differences discussed here are summarized in Figure 5.1.

Because the political situation in many countries has been fluid, placing them once and for all in a specific category does not always work. The classification presented in Table 5.2 should be taken with a grain of salt. Those who know the political history of the individual countries may have comments on this listing. More important than the number of countries in each box, however, is the variation that exists in African regime formation. What matters here are the variable conditions in which efforts at promoting democratic development must be carried out. Two things nonetheless deserve mention here. The first is that the number of countries that have a stable post-independence record is slightly higher (twenty-six) than those that have experienced disruptive coups or civil wars (twenty-three). When it comes to party system, the number of countries that permitted more than one party at independence is greater (thirty-four) than those that insisted on an inclusivist party monopoly (fifteen). The full list of countries can be found in the table below.

Patterns of governance, regardless of classification, have changed little since independence. Overall, they have remained stable, and political turbulence typically occurs within an already dominant type. For example, despite attempted coups and civil violence, Kenya has continued to be clientelist, Tanzania monopolist-movemental, and Cameroon neo-patrimonial and fractured. At the same time, countries like Benin, Liberia, and Sudan may be harder to pin down because of the political changes that have occurred since independence. As Carboni and Raleigh (2021) have noted with reference to the region's many autocratic states, political change comes in cycles – not through rebellion or revolution but through elite competition consisting of accommodation and consolidation that ultimately ends up in fragmentation and crisis. In countries like Mali, Somalia, and South Sudan this cyclical change has reached a true crisis point where they are now best described as "ungovernable states", a fifth category to be added to the four in Table 5.2. In a few instances, like Liberia and Rwanda, which both suffered from a devastating civil war, government has regained control and embarked on a modernization trajectory, but as indicated earlier, conflicts have continued albeit in fewer countries.

The important point here is that African countries have developed these regime types on their own in response to the challenges of managing the state-nation. This process was especially volatile during the first three decades after independence when African leaders

Table 5.2 *African countries organized according to governance regime, 2019*

| Type of regime | Countries |
|---|---|
| Clientelist-competitive | Botswana, Cape Verde, Gabon, Gambia, Ghana, Kenya, Lesotho, Mauritius, Namibia, Senegal, Seychelles, Sudan, Zambia (13) |
| Monopolist-movemental | Guinea, Guinea-Bissau, Malawi, Mali, Mozambique, São Tomé and Principe, South Sudan, Tanzania, Zimbabwe (9) |
| Neo-patrimonial-fractured | Benin, Burkina Faso, Burundi, Cameroon, Central African Republic, Chad, Comoros, Congo Republic, Democratic Republic of the Congo, Djibouti, Equatorial Guinea, Ivory Coast, Liberia, Mauritania, Nigeria, Sierra Leone, Somalia, Swaziland, Togo, Uganda (20) |
| Authoritarian-modernizing | Angola, Eritrea, Ethiopia, Madagascar, Niger, Rwanda (6) |

*Source:* Author; figures guiding the classification taken from Varieties of Democracy Annual Report (2019)

influenced by political euphoria easily became overambitious and engaged in discretionary uses of power. For example, between 1960 and 1990, of the twenty-five heads of state who lost power, only one (Aden Abdullah Dar of Somalia) lost it through an election. After 1990, the record is less alarming: of the sixty-seven coup attempts, thirty were successful. Equally important, however, coup makers did not suspend constitutions as they had in previous decades. Popular resistance and diplomatic objections contributed to limit their options to act. Despite volatility, African countries have also made strides in the pursuit of the rule of law. Between 1960 and 1990 no less than 130 constitutions (that is roughly 3 per country) were thrown out. Since then, as many as 48 new constitutions have been adopted and they have proved resilient. Even countries that did not draft a new one, like Tanzania, made changes to their old ones. Although regimes are still in the making there is evidence throughout the continent of growing institutionalization.

## 5.4   AFRICAN REGIMES AND DEMOCRACY

Without the political economy of more developed regions and lacking the civic tradition of Western countries, a prime issue of political development in Africa is how democratic values can be accommodated within the regimes that African leaders are trying to build. What difference does African regime type make for democratization?

Using the 2018 scores provided by the Varieties of Democracy Index on the degree of liberal democracy in African countries, it is clear that most African countries leave little room for democracy. Overall, however, those that have a clientelist-competitive regime score significantly higher on liberal democracy than the other three types with the authoritarian-modernizing group of countries at the bottom. This confirms that many Africans see a choice between development and democracy, quite contrary to the current mainstream view in both academic and policy circles that democracy is a prerequisite for development. Thanks to the Afrobarometer we know that there is an unfulfilled demand for democracy among ordinary people in Africa (Bratton and Houessou 2014), but a combination of complex governance imperatives and a lack of commitment to democratic norms within the political elite means that the best chances for democracy to take hold in Africa is where political competition generates a response to these demands, as indicated in Table 5.3.

Because Africa's struggle for democracy did not begin in the 1990s but in the 1950s during the global second wave of democratization, understanding what happens with democracy in Africa today involves examining political development and the degree of openness that was permitted by the first post-independence government. Legacies from that time have been influential in many countries to this day. Generally, the clientelist- competitive category tends to be more capable of incorporating civil and political rights than

Table 5.3 *Liberal democracy scores by African regime type*

| Regime type/country | Score | Regime type/country | Score |
|---|---|---|---|
| *Clientelist-competitive* (14) | | *Neo-patrimonial-fractured* (20) | |
| Cape Verde | 0.715 | Benin | 0.673 |
| Mauritius | 0.696 | Burkina Faso | 0.503 |
| South Africa | 0.622 | Liberia | 0.490 |
| Namibia | 0.578 | Nigeria | 0.451 |
| Senegal | 0.577 | Sierra Leone | 0.372 |
| Botswana | 0.576 | Côte d'Ivoire | 0.369 |
| Ghana | 0.537 | Uganda | 0.279 |
| Seychelles | 0.452 | Comoros | 0.252 |
| Lesotho | 0.424 | Togo | 0.240 |
| Kenya | 0.333 | Central African Republic | 0.232 |
| Gambia | 0.296 | Mauritania | 0.158 |
| Gabon | 0.287 | Cameroon | 0.154 |
| Zambia | 0.276 | Somalia | 0.138 |
| Sudan | 0.106 | Djibouti | 0.126 |
| **Average** | **0.480** | Congo | 0.110 |
| | | Democratic Republic of Congo | 0.104 |
| *Monopolist-movemental* (9) | | Swaziland | 0.100 |
| São Tomé and Principe | 0.609 | Chad | 0.094 |
| Malawi | 0.474 | Burundi | 0.055 |
| Mali | 0.442 | Equatorial Guinea | 0.053 |
| Tanzania | 0.386 | **Average** | **0.250** |
| Mozambique | 0.327 | | |
| Guinea-Bissau | 0.316 | *Authoritarian-modernizing* (6) | |
| Guinea | 0.214 | Niger | 0.376 |
| Zimbabwe | 0.205 | Madagascar | 0.263 |
| South Sudan | 0.058 | Rwanda | 0.205 |
| **Average** | **0.337** | Angola | 0.141 |
| | | Ethiopia | 0.107 |
| | | Eritrea | 0.016 |
| | | **Average** | **0.185** |

Legend: 1.0 = top; 0.0 = bottom
*Source:* Author

their monopolist-movemental counterparts. The irony of the African governance context is that a strong party system does not guarantee democracy, especially if it is dominated by an inclusivist mass party. Such parties have monopolized power and marginalized opposition parties and civil society organizations, Tanzania and Zimbabwe being cases in point. In contrast, in countries where parties are weak, leaders have little choice but to engage in transactions that hold power in balance, Kenya being a prime example.

The scores in Table 5.3 tell a lot about African governance that a focus on democracy alone misses. First, they highlight the fact that peaceful development since independence has been a main factor in facilitating the response to demands for more democracy. Both clientelist- competitive and monopolist-movemental regimes score higher than those that suffered from conflict and violence. The former, however, also scores higher than the latter, suggesting that a pluralist approach to political development at independence helped the adaptation to democracy in the early 1990s.

The two former settler colonies, South Africa and Kenya, are among the highest scorers because democratization has been a fight against an enemy within. The presence of white settlers trying to monopolize power became a real target in the transition to a democratic regime for all. Neither the African National Congress (ANC) in South Africa nor the Keny African National Union (KANU) in Kenya became a party capable of monopolizing politics. Minority parties developed during the struggle for independence (or majority rule as in South Africa) and their legacy lived on to facilitate the transition to a multi-party system in the 1990s. In this respect, Africa is similar to Latin America as well as the Middle East and North Africa, where democratization in recent decades has been shaped by what happened way back in the middle of the last century (Waldner 2017).

The data from the Peace Research Institute in Oslo (Bakken and Rustad 2018) provide evidence that countries that have lived through a period of conflict and violence after independence have generally had greater problems of making democracy work on a sustainable basis. Some of them have bounced back from chaos to choose between one of two routes. One is the institutionalization of autocratic rule, typically in a militarist fashion. Their rationale has been that only under military and autocratic rule will the country be able to recover and develop. Rwanda and Ethiopia are examples of countries that have chosen this route. As Table 5.3 confirms, their democracy score is generally lower than that of the other three categories.

Others have opted for a civilian route to manage what in most cases have been fractured societies. Getting back to civilian rule has often proceeded only with the permission of the army as in Nigeria or with the assistance of external bodies as in the cases of Liberia and Sierra Leone. The memory and experience of the killings have no doubt played a role in pushing these countries towards democracy, but the scores of countries in this category vary a lot and the majority find themselves a long way away from institutionalizing a democratic element in their governance. Because these countries are fractured along cleavage lines that tend to go deep, they are also fragile. Salvation has been sought in a strong leader who can refer to a heroic act such as overthrowing a brutal leader or ending a civil war as a justification for the ability to hold the state-nation together. These charismatic leaders, however, have themselves been tempted to remain in power for as long as possible, for example, by changing the constitutional rule of a two-term limit. The result is that wherever a charismatic leader has overstayed his time in power and his role has become neo-patrimonial, the fractured nature of society works against institutionalizing democratic principles. As Kiiza et al. (2008) noted with reference to Uganda, while the government has allowed for regular elections, it has curbed democratic rights that enable other political actors to exercise influence on public opinion. Across Africa, parties in opposition and civil society activism have been the first to suffer as the personalization of power is extended. The denial of civil and political rights occurs in the other governance regimes as well, especially monopolist-movemental and authoritarian-modernizing regimes, but in the latter two a substantive rationale such as "unity is necessary for development" is usually offered to justify the monopoly of power. Wherever else neo-patrimonial leaders reign, the argumentation for hanging on to power rests on much flimsier grounds. For example, people become increasingly less convinced about the indispensability of their leader. Still, the transition from personal to institutionalized rule remains a challenge (Levy 2014). Because societies are fractured there is no spontaneous sense that everyone is equal and that rights apply to all. The political dynamic usually whips up a zero-sum game sentiment with the opposition, fighting for its chance to "chop", to borrow an expression from Ghana suggesting that only some groups or communities are allowed to share the table at the same time (Lindberg 2003).

Universalism is a troublesome concept in all four types of governance regime in Africa, but it tends to become especially contested in countries where neo-patrimonialism is strong. It generates a "we-versus-them" feeling that limits the extension of political rights only to those who are on the inside. When a new group comes to power, its members tend to apply the same logic. Asked to define "democracy", only four out of ten Afrobarometer respondents mentioned "freedom" as part of its essence, leading Bratton (2010) to worry about the equivalences – and validity – of survey responses to questions that may take on a different meaning dependent on culture and history. As he argues, there are ways out of this dilemma, but the point here is that as a key concept like democracy travels across cultures it lands in each place with a different face. As shown here, there is a difference in terms of how governance regimes respond. The more competitive systems demonstrate greater acceptance than those that are monolithic, but competition or rivalry also becomes a threat in countries where the state-nation project is not already resting on a lasting political settlement, as the neo-patrimonial-fractured type illustrates most starkly.

## 5.5   INSTITUTIONS AS BUILDING BLOCKS

Institutions are the building blocks that make up the regime. Comparative analysis of institutions typically starts from the premise that they are rules or norms that serve as guide for human choice and behaviour. Douglass North (1991:97), whose work has been especially influential, defines institutions as "the humanly devised constraints that structure political, economic and social interaction". His work has been interpreted and used in different ways. Economists such as Acemoglu and Robinson (2012) have generally been satisfied with applying the concept to market behaviour. For example, institutions set limits for how consumers act and make their choices. This "thin" version of institution implies that it is relatively easy to create and change. It has become popular especially in international donor circles with their demand for change in economic regulations. The consequence is an overestimation of the role of institutions. An extensive "grey" literature devoted to "institution-building" and "institutional capacity development" confirms the problematic nature of these donor-funded efforts (e.g., Andrews et al. 2012; Carneiro et al. 2015). One of its main points is that institution-building or institutional reform is treated as if it is a matter of learning a new "text", more like the theoretical than the practical part of the exam to get a driving licence. The fact that capacity-building projects tend to be carried out in a hotel or conference hall, a setting far removed from where institutional practices typically take place, reinforces this metaphor. What participants learn from these capacity-enhancing sessions is not immediately practicable in their everyday institutional milieu where they must consider a range of other factors before they regularize their behaviour. What has not been sufficiently acknowledged in this literature is that institutions generally arise as a product of social interaction, individuals learning from each other "on the job". Alternatively, people may learn from their personal experience, their practice. As several studies have shown, donor-funded projects may have succeeded in imparting new knowledge but have fallen short of changing cultural norms, the stuff on which institutions feed (Booth 2011; World Bank 2011; Levy and Walton 2013).

The experience with using institutions as an explanatory variable needs to be revisited. The notion of institutions as formal rules tends to limit what they are all about. They are not just formalized and static. They are living mechanisms that mirror human habits. It is these habits that sustain rules – making institutions the guide to rightful action that we too often take for granted rather than bother to critically analyse. The informality of institutions as embedded in human consciousness is a more helpful way of approaching political systems where regimes are still in the making and political actors are searching for the right blend of norms to guide politics and development. As Berk and Galvan (2009) argue, the default position of rules is not equilibrium but its opposite. Rules or institutions are constantly at the whim of our habits. Their fate, therefore, depends on how we approach them in our daily conduct. For example, there is no reason to assume that people will automatically embrace democratic norms without first having had a personal experience to foster it. Already developed societies provide such an experience in both micro and macro settings – family, school, political parties, and so on. Once a law is passed, citizens take note and make sure they follow it. In many countries around the world, such law abidance does not exist because prevailing habits and preferred behaviour are out of sync. To change that, human habits need to be challenged. To be successful, such challenges must be organized as part of the ongoing political process, for example, in the form of creative deliberations that address the collective experience of a crucial event. Opportunities to change institutions, therefore, do not exist just anywhere or just at any time. Certainly, the seminar room or conference hall is not a very suitable location for attempting such changes. This point is crucial for understanding the prospects for regime change in volatile political systems like those in Africa.

## 5.6 CONCLUSIONS

Managing multi-ethnic relations in the African state-nation context leaves limited room for democracy. Research that focuses on assessing country performances from the vantage point of already developed and democratic societies misses the real challenge of African governance. It overlooks that African governments are engaged in building regimes under strenuous conditions such as poverty and deep social cleavages that do not easily produce positive-sum outcomes. These conditions put limits to what political leaders can do with outside advice or support. Low democracy scores cannot be explained only with reference to corrupt or autocratic leadership. That may be part of the story, but structural factors are equally important in explaining why the space for democracy in African countries is limited and requires struggle to institutionalize. The relevant criterion for assessing African governance, therefore, is not how much farther they have to go to become full democracies but rather how far they have travelled to incorporate democratic norms and values into their governance systems. Unlike most other countries of the world where statehood can be taken for granted, African leaders are still struggling to institutionalize a normative framework for managing statehood and practising statecraft all at one and the same time. Success in this complicated endeavour that Achille Mbembe (2021) characterizes as "an experience of emergence and uprising" depends more on how far prevailing local habits are being challenged than on learning the intricacies of an imported model of democracy.

# 6 Parties and Ideology

## 6.1 INTRODUCTION

Political parties play an important role in mobilizing public opinion and articulating ideas that make their way into policy. Their ideology is their "brand" and gives them identity. In a competitive political environment parties use their identity to carve out a distinct position in the public policy space. In the established democracies in Western countries this space is defined in left–right terms and shaped by underlying socio-economic factors. The relative constancy and stability of the party system have long characterized mainstream Comparative Politics research on the subject. This connection between ideology, party organization, and the emergence of a durable party system is less directly applicable to the African situation because countries lack the social base that holds the party system in check. This chapter identifies the main strands of theorizing in the field and demonstrates how they tend to overlook the specific features of political parties in Africa and the party systems they have spawned.

Formed by groups of people to contest and exercise state power, political parties put life into regime. They do so in different ways, such as by complying, to render it legitimacy; by challenging, to create showdowns; and by calling for reform, to encourage public deliberation. Political parties, therefore, pursue many objectives, sometimes at once. What they have in common is their anchoring in a country's social formations.

## 6.2 CLEAVAGES AND PARTIES

Where social cleavages follow class lines, parties tend to form accordingly. Economic development in Europe and the Americas in the last hundred years has generated party systems around competing economic interests fuelled by the permeation of a market economy. These largely class-based parties are rooted in stable positions on public issues, giving politics a high degree of predictability and scope for positive-sum negotiations. This equilibrium has been threatened in recent years by the emergence of political parties based on social identity. Economic production is no longer the sole force driving party formation and party development; so too are identity criteria like race and religion. As is evident from recent trends in the United States and European countries like Italy, Poland, and Hungary, when such parties become influential, politics easily turns into zero-sum games of "us" against "them" (Mudde and Kaltwasser 2012). Comparative Politics theorizing is slowly adjusting to this illiberal (if not post-liberal!) tendency although it remains analysed through a democratic theory lens.

African political parties have a different origin and trajectory and do not easily fit into the theoretical frameworks that have guided party research in Europe (Erdmann 2004). Although the parties may have begun in the colonial metropoles – especially true for the former French territories – once the struggle for independence began in earnest this legacy was quickly abandoned in favour of a nationalist ideology and organization. It became "we Africans" against "them the former oppressors". For the nationalists the enemy was real, and the struggle produced movements rather than formally organized political parties. After independence, private sector development was treated with suspicion and trade unions were banned or brought under direct control of ruling parties. The ideological seeds of a political system organized along the lines of economic interest were left to perish. Instead, African leaders adopted an international redistributive logic translating into forms of "payback" like foreign aid for Africa's historic contribution to the development of Europe and the Americas through slavery and for the damage colonialism inflicted on African society. These leaders adopted different versions of socialism to convey their outlook in language that would be universally understood (Brockway 1963; Friedland and Rosberg 1964; Mwansasu and Pratt 1979). Because these ideologies lacked roots in productive activities and were called upon to serve nationalist rather than social class objectives, they faded in the post-independence political environment. Several African leaders like Kwame Nkrumah of Ghana and Modibo Keita of Mali who had been strong anti-colonial champions paid the price of being overthrown while in office. Since the experience of these early days, political parties have been careful in embracing ideology. Their practice has become pragmatic and transactional, ideology being confined to critiques of the colonial legacy and its post-colonial manifestations.

## 6.3   DOMINANT THEORIZING THEMES

Comparative Politics has largely taken for granted the thesis, first systematically argued by Schattschneider (1942), that political parties created democracy and it is difficult to see it function without them. Mainstream research has covered a range of factors that shape their role as instruments of sustaining democratic forms of governance. In recent decades, however, questions have been raised about their role as representative organs, with opinion polls in developed countries showing their decline in legitimacy among citizens (Keman 2014; van Biezen and Poguntke 2014). To better understand political parties in societies undergoing social transformation, an overview of how parties have evolved with respect to key functions may be more instructive than referring to current trends in Europe and America. This overview is organized around three issues that reflect trends in Comparative Politics research on political parties, their (1) origin, (2) function, and (3) impact.

### 6.3.1   Origin

The most important point about the origin of political parties in already established democracies is that they began as elite groupings and only gradually evolved into organizations with a broader membership from among segments of the population. This sequencing in

party development coincided with the introduction of universal suffrage at the beginning of the twentieth century. As Duverger (1954)
noted in his seminal analysis of political parties, the elite parties
tended to be weakly organized and pragmatic in orientation, leaving
individuals pretty much free to act at will without violating party
discipline. Party action was largely confined to the parliamentary
arena and leaders acquired their reputation as much from impressive
oratory in the legislature as from interaction with party followers.

The emergence of mass parties did indeed coincide with the
introduction of universal suffrage but equally important is that
European society had already gone through an industrial revolution
that brought large numbers of people into urban centres and thereby
laid the foundation for the creation of cadre parties with mass following. With large numbers of workers living in crowded quarters they
could quite easily be mobilized into parties calling for their working
and living conditions to be improved. These parties, whether socialist or communist, were a logical response to the dramatic transformation in social structures that followed the change from agrarian to
industrial society. Existing parties that had started as elite groupings
had to reinvent themselves, notably by reaching out to the electorate
in new and more organized ways. What happened to the party system
in the first half of the twentieth century was critical for subsequent
political developments, as confirmed by Lipset and Rokkan (1967) in
their analysis of the relation between social cleavage, party system,
and voter alignment in Western European democracies. Their work
illustrated the high degree of party loyalty and stability in the electorate that continued to dominate the political scene in Europe during
the twentieth century (Bartolini and Mair 1990). It was only at the
end of the century that these alignments were challenged by the rise
of parties championing new causes like the environment and cultural
identity, prompting analysts to argue that voters were beginning to
make a real choice rather than just following a tradition of voting for
the same party from one election to the next (Rose and McAllister
1986; Mair 1997; Kriesi 1998; Dalton and Wattenberg 2003).

The European experience with party development shows two things that are important for comparative political analysis. The first is that social structures are key determinants of party systems and their evolution. The new parties in Europe at the end of the last century reflected the emergence of a post-modernist society in which lifestyles – and livelihoods – are different from those hundred years earlier when the old parties grew into organizations with influence over voters and policies. The second point is that it matters when parties were born. They reflect the times and circumstances when they first came about. This point is also made with reference to Latin America by Mainwaring and Zoco (2007), who argue that it is a more important determinant of inter-party competition than the length of time that a party has been in existence. Waldner (2017) has made a similar observation with reference to party legacies in the Middle East and North Africa, showing that features dating back to the mid-twentieth century are still alive in party composition and orientation.

### 6.3.2   Function

While a focus on the origin emphasizes the study of parties as dependent variables, that is, as products of development in society at large, viewing them in a functionalist perspective highlights their role as independent institutions affecting development and the destiny of society. Comparative political studies of their role in society have focused on their three main functions: (1) to compete for support in the electorate to acquire a popular "base", (2) to run for government office, that is, to gain control of key instruments of power, and (3) to pursue policies that appeal to voters and give them legitimacy as officeholders. Each of these functions occurs in a specific institutional context: (1) chasing the vote within an electoral system; (2) running for office in a governmental system; and (3) pursuing policy within a policy space.

Political parties in democracies function within a party system. As such, they are part of a whole based on a pluralist consensus. How political parties have crystallized into systems of equilibrium, where each one pursues its own agenda while also respecting its opposition, is laid out in detail by Giovanni Sartori (1976). He links this evolution to freedom of expression and the opportunity that it gives for parties to serve as instruments of political representation. Party systems, however, do not arise in a vacuum. An especially important factor determining how they function is the type of electoral system within which they must perform. The link between party and electoral system has been another important topic of research in Comparative Politics ever since Maurice Duverger (1954) concluded his analysis of two-party and multi-party systems in Western democracies. He linked the former with electoral systems based on single-member districts and a plural majority for victory and the latter with an electoral system based on multi-member districts and a proportional allocation of seats in the legislature. Duverger's observation was for some time considered the closest Comparative Politics had come to having a "law", that is, a finding that could be taken for granted when tested in different political systems. As more research has been conducted in Western Europe and increasingly in other regions of the world, "Duverger's Law" has proved to be too simple and insufficient to cover the full variation of party systems. Sartori (1976) was the first to show how party systems could be more comprehensively analysed taking into consideration whether they foster a centrifugal or centripetal type of politics. He noted that parties occupy policy space on a left–right ideological continuum and therefore are locked into positions from which they can deviate only at risk of losing their core support. The idea that two-party systems automatically converge centripetally towards the centre of this continuum while multi-party systems move in a centrifugal fashion to positions at its extreme ends was later called into question by research on smaller European countries. Arend Lijphart's (1977, 1984) study of the Netherlands showed that multi-party systems, even when based on vertical faith cleavages, may indeed converge towards a form of "consociational democracy" in equilibrium.

In the last three decades the tone and orientation in research on political parties have shifted from focusing on the equilibrium of the party system to its volatility (Dalton and Wattenberg 2002). There are two factors that have brought about this change in research on both Europe and Latin America. One is the downside of convergence. Political parties that have become part of the "establishment" have simultaneously been locked into a policy space that makes them less sensitive to the new issues that arise to challenge the middle ground. These issues such as climate, environment, gender, and nationalism have instead been domesticated by new political parties, often started as social movements. The presence of these new parties has not necessarily turned into centrifugal political tendencies, but it has made the party system more volatile and much less predictable (Mainwaring 2018). The second factor is the decline in party membership, which has happened especially in the older parties that have dominated politics for generations. Thus, while the "traditional" parties are losing ground, the new parties are gaining support (van Biezen and Poguntke 2014). This has been especially true for those with a populist message like the Five Star Movement in Italy and the Best Party in Iceland. These parties call into question the legitimacy of the others and, in effect, the liberal democratic system at large. It is not clear how long the influence of these parties will last, but there is no doubt that their existence has changed both politics and Comparative Politics research.

### 6.3.3 Impact

How effective are political parties? What is their impact? These questions have been addressed primarily in a democracy context. When the original elite parties evolved into mass organizations with their own ideology and hierarchy, critics on both the right and the left raised the alarm. Lockean liberals saw these political parties as constraining individual freedom, forcing people to give it up in the interest of party loyalty. Believers in Rousseau's "General Will" argued that political parties would be divisive and pose a threat to the unity of the then emerging nation-states in Europe. Both criticisms contain a grain of truth, but with the institutionalization of stable party systems, the strength of these objections gradually declined. Instead of being viewed as voluntary organizations of citizens with the objective of pursuing their own interest over that of the nation at large, the functionalist perspective that took hold in the period after the Second World War treated parties as institutions essential for democratic governance. Anthony Downs (1957), with his economic theory of democracy, was especially influential in laying the foundation for a shift from normative to formal theory linked, for example, to investigations using scientific sampling and related statistical methods. It is within such a framework that most research on assessing the role of political parties in democracies has been pursued lately. It has addressed issues such as what difference the number of political parties, their length of time in existence, and their degree of effective institutionalization make to democracy. An important contribution was the idea that the number of parties is not informative without first assessing their relative strength (Laakso and Taagepera 1979). Their research of the party systems in Western Europe triggered a series of follow-up studies (e.g., Coppedge 1994; Dunleavy and Boucek 2003). The conclusion seems to be that the notion of "effective party" makes sense in explaining the nature of democratic governance in established democracies. In Western Europe, the number or strength, however, is less important than the readiness within individual parties to form alliances or coalitions (Kitschelt 1999). For example, Sweden has seven effective political parties belonging to two opposing alliances that compete for control of the political middle, a situation that is also found in the other Nordic countries (Gilljam and Oscarsson 1996). Readiness to engage in programmatic negotiations within a system of pluralist consensus is what sets these Western European democracies apart. The conclusion, therefore, is that individual parties make no direct contribution of their own, but as managers of the party system as an indispensable middle ground between society and state, they do have an impact on the quality of democracy in these countries. Studies of political parties in the new democracies in Eastern Europe show that they have little influence

on democracy because they are clientelist and hence weakly institutionalized (Webb and White 2007). Randall (2007) confirms that
parties in new democracies do not add to the overall legitimacy of
the political system and are often its weakest link. This observation
prompts a specific look at parties in Africa.

## 6.4   POLITICAL PARTIES IN AFRICA

African political parties began to develop in earnest as part of the
second wave of democratization after the end of the Second World
War. Their programmes had an identical principal objective: to gain
political independence. While the colonial powers during this period
tried to "teach" their African subjects the practice of democracy
through participation in local governance, nationalist leaders had a
more radical agenda focused on independence. Individual freedom
was side-lined in favour of a communitarian nationalism. As a result,
liberally oriented parties were either incorporated into the dominant
nationalist movement or outright banned by the state. The legacy of
this early period, however, continued to live on in Africa, and like
Waldner (2017) noted with reference to the Middle East and North
Africa, it helped shape the developments as the third wave of democratization set in. Thus, the countries that came to independence with
a competitive party system scored higher on democracy in 2018 than
those who did so under a one-party movement structure (Hyden and
Kristensen 2019). Party developments in Africa have some features
that are common with other developing regions, but they are also
quite different from the political party research discussed earlier. The
differences are summarized in Table 6.1.

Although there were parties in Europe and the Americas before
modernization that functioned as platforms for elite groups to arrive
at legislative consensus, the cadre parties based on formal membership arrived on the political scene only after society had undergone
a state-driven transformation with social cleavages along the lines
of rivalling economic interests, as indicated earlier. Political parties
were never drivers of this process but served as aggregators of these

Table 6.1 *Comparison of political parties in established democracies and sub-Saharan Africa*

| Variable | Established democracies | Sub-Saharan Africa |
|---|---|---|
| Time of origin | After modernization | Before modernization |
| Trajectory | Gradual evolution | Arduous evolution |
| Membership | Limited but committed | Large but fluid |
| Function | Balancing multiple functions | Prioritizing state capture |
| Positioning | Within specific domestic policy space | Open-ended, driven by external policy inputs |
| Effect | Indirect but effective | Direct but ineffective |

*Source:* Author

interests within the political system. Political parties in Africa, in contrast, originated before such a transformation had taken place. Attempts by the colonial powers to modernize African societies fell short of their objective, and nationalist leaders put a halt to much of it by adopting an anti-colonial stand. This placed these leaders in a dilemma. To earn legitimacy, they needed to juggle two tasks in one go: (1) prove their ability to lead in a progressive manner and (2) mark their distance from the colonial past. This meant they searched for ideological inspiration from other modernization "laggards" like the Soviet Union and China. Even though these parties at least for brief periods of time mobilized large numbers of people to support their effort, they failed in their revolutionary ambitions. African societies, as discussed in previous chapters, lack the socio-economic dynamic that was present in countries that had already been restructured by either an agrarian or an industrial revolution. After some time, therefore, party ideological decrees became nothing more than empty phrases, mobilization campaigns no more than instant events. The idea that the party must play a key role ended with political leaders viewing state capture as a legitimate pursuit. In addition to privileging party leaders with power and perks, it provided followers with proof that the party was serious about building the new nation, as Zolberg (1966) explains in his account of how political order was created in West Africa and corroborated by Hyden (1969) in his study of how the nation was built in Tanzania. Instead of being able to ride the wave of modernization, as happened in Europe and the Americas, political parties in Africa took on the heavy burden of social transformation, viewing it as crucial for their legitimacy. They did so, however, without fully appreciating the structural obstacles their own society was posing.

Six decades later it is clear that when it comes to post-independence development, those parties that took on this task with true assiduity – those that Coleman and Rosberg (1964) labelled "revolutionary-centralizing" – have generally fared less well than their "pragmatic-pluralist" counterparts. The latter type may have appeared weak in the years immediately after independence, but because they allowed an open economy to serve as a driver of change, many of them, such as Botswana, Kenya, Mauritius, Nigeria, and South Africa, are today economically ahead of most other countries in the region. Their relative success, however, can hardly be attributed to their political parties. Both party types have been quite ineffective, the first because of adopting a dominant or absolutist role, pre-empting the emergence of a stable political system, the second because of failing to develop into formal and reliable structures and instead relying on personalized informal arrangements.

The inference, therefore, is that party formation and development has been a challenging process in African countries (Randall and Svåsand 2002). As LeBas (2011) argues, the process has been determined by how well parties have been able to mobilize resources and identify themselves vis-à-vis other parties. This effort has been constrained by the weakness of corporate actors and a social setting in which drawing a line other than between communities of consumption makes little sense as long-term strategy. This is a special challenge for opposition parties that need to sustain a form of activism to justify their existence. Kuenzi and Lambright (2001), who studied party institutionalization a decade into the Third Wave, found that it was generally much lower than in Latin America. Using the same criteria that Mainwaring and Scully (1995) had developed for the latter region, they drew two important and related conclusions. The first is that the short length of exposure to democracy explains the low levels in Africa, the second that only a handful of countries (with one exception all of them in southern Africa) demonstrate a convincing degree of institutionalization with respect to (1) regularity of party competition, (2) the extent to which parties manifest roots in society, and (3) the extent to which citizens and organized interests perceive parties and elections as means of determining who governs. This state of affairs does not bode well for democratic development in the region, a point that has also been argued by Mozzafar and Scarritt (2005).

While it is doubtful that political parties contribute to democracy in Africa, they still have a presence that cannot be ignored. Krönke et al. (2020) have measured the presence of political parties by asking respondents with which party they most identify. Their Party Presence Index provides at least two insights that challenge previous findings. The first is that opposition parties, even if they may be underfunded, are organized at different sub-national levels with local support. Their second finding is that political parties are not so much present in the more economically developed countries of the region as they are in island states and other small and less developed countries like Liberia, Sierra Leone, and Uganda. The degree of party presence correlates with demographic density, which is true also for a territorially large place such as Tanzania where the population is concentrated in clusters across the country. Even if parties may have a presence in local districts, the question is, what difference does party institutionalization make to politics? Does it raise political consciousness? Does it sharpen ideological or policy differences?

In societies where policy positions are not grounded in organized economic interest groups, ideology is at best a thin veneer. Where the primary objective of political parties is state capture, there is no sense of a public good to share with others. Policy implementation favours "insiders". If your community is not represented in government, the chances are slim that policies will benefit your group. As already mentioned, in pre-agrarian society contexts, elections are not fought over ideological or policy differences as much as about who gets a seat at the table with access to the public purse (Lindberg 2003). It is no surprise, therefore, that political parties reflect the social cleavages of individual countries, such as whether there is a dominant ethnic group, there are several roughly equal such groups, or there are many small groups. As Sebastian Elischer (2013) points out in his analysis of the political parties in Africa, these circumstances tend to determine whether the party system is dominated by a single party, is competitive, or is built around coalitions of multiple parties. All parties are basically ethnic, representing groups that are not grounded in the economic production process but in structures with a consumption perspective on the political process. Parties may have their own programmes, but they are composed around principles and values reflected in global agreements initiated by the international donor community. The result is that the policy message parties convey is similar and expressed in general terms like "education for all". The parties compete in terms of who make the strongest point within a generally accepted policy preference. It is in this respect that policy pronouncements enter political campaigns. The way that African parties try to influence the minds of voters cannot be compared to that of parties in developed societies, which are grounded in specific policy positions that represent contending economic interests. The result is that although opposition parties need to mark a difference from government policy (LeBas 2011), they do so by racing rather than boxing. Without the rationale that the economic group interest provides politics, the system lacks the dynamic that tends to produce a durable competitive form of multi-party politics (Salih 2003). This is also the reason why political leaders find it easy to justify the one-party system as preferable in Africa. What matters to the voter is picking the party that stands the greatest chance of gaining access to the public purse. If there is only one party, the choice becomes so much easier.

## 6.5 CONCLUSIONS

This chapter has examined how political parties in African countries compare with parties in other regions. The most significant thing they have in common with other developing and democratizing regions is a low level of party institutionalization. The average level in African countries, however, is considerably lower than, for example, in Latin America. Party systems are volatile because political parties tend to be either just personalized factions or dominated by a single organization with little interest in levelling the playing field for other parties. Elections do occasionally produce a change in power, especially in countries with a competitive party system. Such shifts, however, do not typically reflect real differences in policy. Instead, the consequence of a political shift is no more than a rearrangement of communities of consumption competing for access to power and government resources. Political parties do not need ideology to attract followers, nor do donor-initiated policy programmes really differentiate them. Party strategies in Africa, therefore, are built around finding individuals with the qualities to serve as the champion of as many consumption communities as possible. Where state capture is the prime objective, party politics easily becomes both transactional and authoritarian. This form of politics, which has been a dominant feature of African countries since independence, has set limits to a democratic transition, as Doorenspleet and Nijzink (2013) and Riedl (2014) show in their respective treatment of the subject. Above all, it has slowed down the emergence of a political culture infused with democratic values.

# 7 Culture and the Public Sphere

7.1 INTRODUCTION

When Comparative Politics began to take shape within the discipline in the early 1960s, the concept of political culture featured prominently in how political development might be best understood. In one of the defining contributions, Pye and Verba (1965) argued that in the final analysis the problems of political development revolve around the relationship between the political culture, the authoritative structure, and the general political process. In their functionalist perspective, political culture was defined as the sum of views, values, and attitudes people hold towards the political system. Over time, with the decline of functionalism and the rise of positivist theory, political culture was marginalized and reduced to the positive data of experience, for example, interview surveys. Drawing conclusions about national political cultures using such surveys, however, is problematic, and following influences from hermeneutics, notably the works of Jürgen Habermas (1981), the concept has been reinvented with a focus on discourse and empowerment. This involves accepting the public sphere as the prime forum for political discourse and a recognition of public opinion as a driving force in shaping and changing political culture.

This chapter traces the evolution of the study of political culture in mainstream Comparative Politics. It emphasizes the role that political culture has been playing as an explanatory variable as illustrated, for example, in the following two influential theses: (1) modern values produce development and (2) democratic values produce good governance. Western countries have viewed themselves as having embarked on a mission to disseminate these progressive values to the rest of the world. In their approach to political culture in Africa, political scientists, therefore, have concurred with the view that reforms are needed. Originally conceived as "traditional", the initial calls were to make the culture "civic" (Almond and Verba 1963). The same premise has underpinned much survey work as well as more recent research on democratization. In placing research on African political culture in its wider Comparative Politics context, the chapter highlights why tackling it through Western eyes has its limits. As Cheeseman (2015) notes in his comprehensive overview of success and failure in the region's effort to democratize, too little attention has been paid to the views that Africans themselves hold about the subject. This chapter adds further insights into what the literature has so far largely overlooked.

## 7.2 POLITICAL CULTURE IN COMPARATIVE POLITICS

Pye (1967) provided the first authoritative definition of political culture, referring to it as the shared values, attitudes, and sentiments that people belonging to a community, typically a nation, hold towards the system by which they are governed. Thus, it refers to aggregate sentiments, values, and views directed towards the political system at large. Subsequent use of the concept has largely adopted a similar position. In this dominant perspective, political culture is not the same as public opinion. The latter is a subset of political culture relating to specific issues or policies. Its role in political culture depends on the extent to which it is sustained by organized efforts. An instant public response to an event does not amount to public opinion, nor do the responses of sampled individuals – even if approached in a regular manner to assess whether their opinions endure or shift. Survey responses, therefore, are only meaningful for the study of political culture – and its contribution to political development – when they reflect or can be related to organized opinion. Wherever this is the case, public opinion is an important determinant of the nature and direction of a country's political culture.

Table 7.1 *Comparison of three approaches to the study of political culture*

| Variable/approach | Functionalist | Positivist | Hermeneutic |
|---|---|---|---|
| Disciplinary origin | Anthropology | Economics | Sociology |
| Level of analysis | Macro | Micro | Meso |
| Theoretical premise | Structural reflection | Aggregation of individual responses | Creative deliberations |
| Principal method | Historical data | Scientific surveys | Discourse analysis |
| Orientation | Evolutionary | Static | Dynamic |
| Validity claim | Reliable sources | Objectivity | Intersubjectivity |

*Source:* Author

Political culture has been the subject of ongoing debate about its role in political development. As suggested earlier, it is possible to identify three theoretical approaches that have been especially influential in shaping this debate: (1) functionalism, (2) positivism, and (3) hermeneutics. What characterizes each approach and how they differ among themselves are summarized in Table 7.1.

Each approach has a deeper philosophical origin that is not listed in the table. Functionalism, for instance, may be traced back to Aristotle and Hobbes, positivism to Auguste Comte and James Mill, and critical theory to Immanuel Kant and Friedrich Hegel. What matters more here is the close relation that political science has with its social science neighbours. Ideas borrowed from these sources have been influential in shaping the debate in Comparative Politics. The feature of this debate that concerns us most directly here is how political culture relates to political development.

### 7.2.1   *Functionalism*

The functionalist perspective rests on a systems theory. Its parts are all interdependent and thus influence each other. As such, the system is more than just the sum of its parts as they work to maintain order and consensus. This was the predominant orientation in the social sciences during the middle of the twentieth century when comparativists tried to find a theoretical foundation for analysing politics across cultures. Political culture was viewed as a product of the political system's structural properties. The more these structures were differentiated, the more developed the system was – and hence the more modern the political culture. With its in-built slant to consensus and order, functionalism was an ideal tool for theorizing political development that responded to the wishes in the United States and Europe at the time to define a positive political trajectory in contrast with the totalitarian vision of the Soviet Union and China. As discussed in Chapter 1, functionalism was married to a theory of social change, more specifically of how countries in Europe and North America became modern. Functionalism gave modernization a level of inevitability because in a systems perspective parts work to make it a progressive force. In the Comparative Politics literature at the time, the process of change was cast in terms of a move from systems relying on traditional authority to those researchers labelled "modern". The latter were Western countries that had evolved into liberal democracies. Western political leaders viewed this as the preferred endpoint of political development. Functionalism rendered it a degree of scientific justification.

Functionalism, while serving like behaviourism as a force in the move towards a "new" political science, eventually became the subject of criticism from many sources. Two are of special relevance here. The first was the reification of abstract structures into real things. Conceived as parts of an abstract political system, structures were empirically treated as agents of change. Modernization was not the result of human willpower but, in a teleological perspective, the outcome of structural dynamics. This structuralist approach made it possible to attribute agency to any political system, a point that at the time was both politically and theoretically significant. Politicians had to accept the sovereignty and freedom of new nations that had previously been colonies but now needed to be treated as autonomous political systems. Comparativists, on their part, needed a universal theory of development for cross-national analysis. Their ethnocentric interpretation of the modernization concept, however, was in the end what undercut the influence of functionalism.

### 7.2.2  Positivism

Positivism was in several respects the direct opposite to functionalism. The unit of analysis was no longer at macro but at micro level. Human agency was prioritized over structure, and scientifically designed opinion surveys became the preferred mode of ascertaining public opinion and political culture. Perhaps the most significant change, however, was the abandonment of the search for the origin of values. Positivism cut this Gordian Knot by positing that human agency is driven by self-interest, whether enlightened or not. This made the question of values moot and the analysis of how people behave and make their choices both straightforward and parsimonious. This mode of analysis became attractive especially in the context of the institutional reform programmes that evolved in the late twentieth century. It downplayed the role of political culture as a developmental variable. Instead, political culture was reported in a static photographic manner, indicating survey response preferences to specific issues rather than their attitude to the wider political system. This aggregation of individual responses was of interest to people in policy circles but lost much of their value to comparativist scholars with a focus on state formation and nation-building.

### 7.2.3  Hermeneutics

Neither functionalism nor positivism really gave political culture its due. It is only with the emergence of hermeneutics that it has risen to prominence as an independent variable. Words matter, so do conversations and discussions, or what Habermas (1981) calls communicative action. What people say in public – and how they do it – has consequences and it reflects their involvement with others. Rationality is not necessarily just an end–means type of calculation centred on self-interest. A complementary communicative rationality that recognizes the influence of experiences and social interaction is equally important. Taking this stand, Habermas could easily have been accused of relativism but his ambition to design a universalist "pragmatics" by focusing on the forms and procedures of public discourse saved him from such an accusation. His analysis, however, landed him in an ethnocentric "trap". His hermeneutic analytical design was too closely derived from the Western European model of bourgeois society in which discourse is the upshot of socially autonomous or "free" individuals interacting in a rational manner. In addition, critics have suggested that his theory is too proceduralist and overestimates the willingness of people to adhere to specific rules for civil discourse (Calhoun 1992).

## 7.3 STREAMS OF DISCOURSE ANALYSIS

Habermas' work on discourse analysis has spun off research on political culture that has become important parts of Comparative Politics. It is possible to identify three streams: (1) the role of media in politics, (2) the significance of deliberation in democracy, and (3) the way political culture can be changed through empowerment campaigns. Each one will be the subject of a brief elaboration here.

### 7.3.1 Role of the Media in Politics

The media role in politics takes many forms, two of which are central to the analysis here. First, the media can define the frames within which a policy debate is conducted. Frames are primarily interpretive schemata through which meaning is made. Actors in the media, when reporting a story, typically weigh which facts to include or emphasize, which sources to cite, and how to present what is "at issue" (Entman 2001). Such choices combine to create a frame that both supports the story and influences interpretation by the public. A second important role that the media play in politics is to serve as venues of public debate. The editorial page or its accompanying space (the op-ed) is at least in liberal media usually open for opposing or independent opinions. Letters to the editor constitute another option to participate in public discourse.

The exact media influence is difficult to track, but Robinson (2001) argues that the media role becomes important in times of political distrust, especially if it is directed against key public institutions or elected leaders (Moy and Scheufele 2000; Norris 2000). In such cases, media intervention can become especially significant in legitimizing a given interpretation of events. By presenting their own narrative, the media may turn into "agenda-setters" (McCombs 2004). Even if the media do not necessarily tell you how to think, they can tell you what to think about. The salience of issues on the media agenda, therefore, affects not only which ones the public consider most important but also how their political or policy preferences are ultimately determined (McCombs 2004).

### 7.3.2   Significance of Deliberative Democracy

The concept of communicative rationality has opened a new perspective and interpretation of democracy. "Deliberative democracy" is today an integral part of Comparative Politics. Its significance is acknowledged, for example, in the data sets on democracy provided by the Varieties of Democracy Institute. As used in comparative analysis the concept refers to the "life" of democracy between elections. While participation in elections involves the use of instrumental or purposive rationality, being involved in politics between elections relies foremost on a communicative rationality, that is, a willingness to discuss and compromise with others within agreed-upon rules – the component of democracy that John Stuart Mill referred to as "government by discussion". It calls attention to how democratic values are institutionalized or how citizens and leaders become democrats. Deliberative democracy rests on the notion that citizens participate as free individuals with a view to sustaining institutions. The crux of the theory is that there can be "no democracy without democrats".

The general aim of deliberative democracy is to provide the most justifiable conception for dealing with moral disagreement in politics (Bessette 1994; Gutman and Thompson 2002; Dryzek 2010). As such, it is an important component of efforts aimed at

fostering democratic development. It promotes the legitimacy of collective decisions in various ways. First, in the ever-present context
of resource scarcity, deliberation can help those who do not get what
they want, or even what they need, to accept the legitimacy of a collective decision. Hard choices become more acceptable if stakeholder
claims have been considered on their merits rather than on the basis
of someone's bargaining power. Second, deliberation also encourages perspectives on public issues that transcend special interests. It
helps to make deliberators generally better informed and aware of the
rationale behind the position of others. It does not imply that they
abandon their position as advocates of specific groups or constituen-
cies, but by taking a broader view of issues in a process in which
moral reasons, not just power, are traded, compromise and consensus
are more likely outcomes. Third, deliberative democracy provides a
forum for correcting mistakes that citizens and officials may make.
This is a response to the all-too-common situation where decisions
are made without complete knowledge or understanding (Lindblom
1959). A well-constituted deliberative forum provides an opportunity
for assessing policy outcomes and learning from what may have gone
wrong, a scenario that is more common than one where everything
went perfectly.

Deliberative democracy has its critics. They follow different
lines, the most important relating to how deliberation can be recon-
ciled with (1) representation, (2) power distribution, and (3) the desire
for change (Bohman 1998; Elster 1998). The first of these issues arises
because Habermas assumed that discourse occurs in the public sphere
located outside the political and administrative spheres with its own
purposive rationality. His view of the public sphere coincides with
what scholars coming out of different theoretical traditions refer to
as "civil society" – the arena where issues tend to be identified as
the initial stage in a broader political and administrative process.
Attempts have been made to develop a theory that builds deliberation into a system of representation, for example, the notion of a
"direct deliberative polyarchy" (Cohen and Sabel 1997). This attempt

to link deliberative to representative democracy has not been very effective in changing the minds of those comparativists who are sceptical towards the concept. They argue that reaching consensus through bargaining and voting is more effective given that time is a scarce commodity and decisions are driven by more considerations than reaching consensus in the public realm (e.g., Braybrooke and Lindblom 1963).

Reconciling deliberative democracy with the power realities in countries around the world is perhaps the biggest challenge facing its advocates. The rules of discourse may make it civil, but they can also be used to exclude people. This happens in two different ways. One is the way the public sphere is defined. Despite the spread of equality as a universal principle, many societies continue to treat some groups as more patriotic or worthier than others, resulting in discriminatory practices that narrow the boundaries of the public sphere. Thus, the consensus that may be built is confined to a community that is not reflective of all social groups. This is evident, for example, in countries with indigenous populations such as the Americas and Australia but also in countries with a growing population of migrants as discussed in Chapter 4 on the state-nation. The other way is when the public sphere may be inclusive in theory, but participation in practice is limited to a few and consensus is built above the heads of the majority. This consensus may be benevolent as, for example, Englund (2006) has shown with reference to activists conducting human rights campaigns in poor countries with little sense of how they are perceived by members of local communities. An elite–mass gap emerges as conventional values are being challenged. Something similar is evident in the populist position in developed societies with its rejection of the "establishment".

### 7.3.3   *Political Culture as Empowerment*

While political culture has its critics and sceptics, it also has its believers and activists. There is an important sub-theme in political culture that is built on the premise that political culture can be used to empower people to change their position in life. It dates back a hundred years to the Italian theorist and activist Antonio Gramsci, who composed his thoughts about empowerment while imprisoned by Mussolini's fascist government between 1922 and his death in 1937. His "notebooks from prison" have subsequently been translated into many languages and published in three volumes in the United States (Gramsci 2011). Although being a Marxian theorist, he disagreed with the orthodox view that the working class would rise because of the depravity it faces under capitalism. Instead, he accepted that workers had bought into the capitalist system. The challenge of the revolutionary, therefore, was to overthrow the hegemony of the whole value system on which society is being ruled. In this way, he accepted that political culture is as important as political economy in determining the direction of society. He, of course, never had a chance to personally experience his theory in practice, but it has remained a source of inspiration for subsequent generations, Marxian as well as non-Marxian.

In recent decades, the empowerment concept has been revived as part of dealing with poverty and underdevelopment. Much of it has been driven by two philosophers and theorists with social justice as their primary concern. Amartya Sen (1999) launched the concept of "development as freedom" and Martha Nussbaum (1999) added her notion of "capabilities". For human life to be fully realized, people must have capabilities to do so. These two theorists battle with the question of whether values are absolute or relative, that is, specific to different cultures. This issue becomes central to their argument that freedom is universal, but capabilities are embedded in cultures that differ. Their way of dealing with this issue is to argue that human development is local but can be facilitated by a roster of capabilities associated with "a good life" as defined in international agreements on human rights and development. Empowerment, therefore, is a matter of creating the right conditions – an enabling environment – in which people in different societies can make progress towards greater freedom and social justice, starting and working within familiar cultural frames. What they need is not a blueprint but a roadmap. This is an issue that has been hotly debated in the international donor community where the political mistake of relying on policy blueprints has been made over and over (Booth 2015).

Another important trend in the theoretical literature on empowerment is related to uplifting the conditions of specific underprivileged groups. The most common target has been women, not only in developing countries but also in more developed societies. Much of it has focused on creating civic space for women's voice to be heard in society (Mansbridge 1999). The need for more female leadership at different levels in society has been another focal point (Kabeer 1994). While much of this literature has had a political economy orientation, many authors have emphasized the importance of transforming the cultural frames within which issues of development are being approached (Inglehart and Norris 2003). With an eye on political action, others argue for an agenda-setting approach to enlarging the political space for achieving greater equality between the genders (Benhabib 2006).

## 7.4  POLITICAL CULTURE IN AFRICA

The comparative study of African politics has come a long way since it was extensively influenced by research on "traditional" values and how they relate to development. Some of these studies became pathbreaking at the time. One was the study of the politics of cultural pluralism by Crawford Young (1976) in which he compared select African and Asian states, drawing the conclusion, for instance, that Nigeria may have more in common with culturally plural countries like India than with many of its African neighbours. What these early studies had in common is that they described and analysed the situation on the ground and problematized political development in a local perspective. They recognized the significance of indigenous African values, views, and sentiments. In short, half a century ago, political culture as constituted in local African conditions was treated as a key variable worthy of comparison across countries not only in Africa but also other developing regions.

Since then, things African have lost their position in comparative analysis. It began with the turn to political economy in the 1980s and the permeation of a public choice approach to the study of not only policy but also politics (e.g., Bates 1981). It encouraged a focus on institutional reform, treating those already on the ground as ineffective and – often – corrupt. What African decision-makers considered as the appropriate manner and context in which to govern their countries in a legitimate manner was branded not good enough by the dominant voices in the international community. Western donors went as far as making the adoption of their own institutional formulas a condition for continued development assistance. This has continued in this century, with the same donors making the adoption of liberal democratic institutions tied to their aid. With no incentive or interest to learn about local values and context, Western donors have missed having a real impact with their democracy aid (Carothers and De Gramont 2013; Hyden and Kristensen 2019).

Nowhere is this more evident than in the efforts to promote the development of a public sphere or civil society. As already noted, the rise of a public sphere in Europe in the nineteenth century relied on venues and platforms where a free debate could take place outside of the political-administrative sphere. Tea and coffee houses in European cities like London, Paris, and Vienna were the forerunners that paved the way for a more institutionalized civic public sphere serving as a complement to an organized political opposition in checking government (Ellis 2004). The rise of the public sphere was facilitated by the social differentiation and stratification that followed in the wake of industrialization and the rise of capitalism. To be successful in society, it was no longer necessary to seek a career in politics. There were plenty of opportunities in finance, commerce, and the professions. As people organized in guilds and associations, they not only promoted their own interest but also shared a public spirit by voluntarily investing in activities supporting others in society. Philanthropy became a mark of respect in these increasingly bourgeois societies. It helped legitimize wealth while at the same time engendering a greater variety and intensity of civic activities that helped strengthen the public sphere (Van Horn Melton 2001).

The creation of a public sphere in African countries is attempted in conditions that differ from Europe. There are few wealthy persons that fill the public space between the local community and the political-administrative establishment. Wealth, therefore, is foremost shared with the local communities from which the wealthy benefit by serving as benefactors. Instead of the rise of a bourgeoisie, wealth in Africa encourages clientelism based on the distribution of patronage (Kramon and Posner 2013; Adebanwi and Obadare 2015; Osei 2018). As Peter Ekeh (1975) was the first to argue, loyalty in African society is not to a civic public sphere but to one based on communal values. This interest in the communal public sphere has developed into research on autochthony, that is, movements that claim citizenship based on being "sons of the soil". This way of politicizing ethnicity goes deep and is a threat to national unity as shown in the cases of Cameroon and Ivory Coast (Geshiere and Nyamnjoh 2000; Geshiere 2009). It would be wrong, however, to assume that only apocalyptic scenarios prevail. As African societies deal with their cleavage issues, there are many formal as well as informal measures that aim at transcending the threats to national unity inherent in ethnicity (MacLean 2010; Gibson and Hoffman 2013).

Measuring participation in politics or deliberation in policy-making is not easy but the Varieties of Democracy Institute provides some information by using its expert survey to assess levels of different aspects of democracy. The 2020 data for deliberative democracy show that, in comparison with other regions of the world, sub-Saharan Africa falls well behind Latin America and Eastern Europe but is ahead of the Middle East and North Africa region. The former two follow the mainstream interpretation of democracy in the past thirty years: a sharp rise in the 1990s and a marked decline around 2020. In contrast, Africa displays a flatter trajectory, with even a small improvement around 2020. Participation measures do not change that interpretation. This is yet another confirmation that

Africa was never affected by the Third Wave of Democratization in a significant manner. There is no sense of loss because there was never much of it in the first place. Instead, the African trajectory centres on extending civic and political space to degrees that they have never enjoyed. This yearning for more democracy is evident in both indices and confirms the data from the Afrobarometer that the demand for democracy in the region is higher than what the political leadership supplies (Bratton and Housseau 2014).

A closer look at the data also reveals that only one third of the African countries qualify for a place in the upper half of these global indices. Ivory Coast is the region's top performer in political participation, Niger in deliberative democracy. Together with Ethiopia, the Democratic Republic of Congo, and Gambia, Niger shows improvement above the scores for the previous year, while Mauritius, Ghana, Benin, and Namibia show a decline. The fall of these "success" cases of democracy in Africa suggests that there may have been an overestimation of what happened in the 1990s when the euphoria of the Third Wave tended to affect expert judgments everywhere. Taken together, these measures suggest that the values, views, and sentiments that make up political culture in African countries rest on a volatile foundation.

A major reason is the weakness of the public sphere. The political-administrative sphere is dominant in terms of both recruitment and agenda-setting. Donor support reinforces its hegemony. There are few, if any, social movements to energize the public sphere, and whatever exists in the form of civil society typically lacks a critical mass of local membership organizations that are strong enough to shape a public opinion on important policy issues. Attempts at agenda-setting in African countries are largely made by international non-governmental organizations. They can count on their financial strength, but they encounter difficulties in helping to build an independent public sphere in the countries where they are present. As highlighted in the 2020 State of Civil Society Report issued by the global alliance of civil society organizations and activists, civil society faces challenges everywhere in the world (CIVICUS 2020). The issues that drive its members globally such as social justice, exclusion, discrimination, and climate change are also present on African activist agendas but have less direct impact on the nature of the public sphere than in other regions. One reason is the monopoly of problem definition that governments seek, often through outright oppression of activism. Another related reason is the continued weakness of civil society organizations to stand up against authority for fear of losing their licence to operate. The one exception here is faith-based organizations, which enjoy a degree of financial autonomy that allows them to criticize government in public (Tshimpaka and Nshimbi 2021). These organizations constitute the still volatile scaffolding of the state that characterizes Africa. The organizational basis for developing a public sphere where issues can be freely debated remains weak. Political culture in African countries continues to be largely void of a civic public sphere. Mainstream as well as social media struggle to keep issues alive, but because of being penalized or outright oppressed, their space for making a difference to the strengthening of a public sphere is significantly constrained in most countries (Mudhai et al. 2009; Hyden and Kristensen 2019). Thus, the hope some years ago that social media would foster a democratic development has remained largely unfilled.

## 7.5  CONCLUSIONS

As this chapter has tried to demonstrate, political culture has had its own identity issues, having initially been treated as just a manifestation of social structures to becoming in recent years itself a driver of change – following unsuccessful efforts by rational choice theorists to get rid of it altogether. Today, it is an important part of the literature related to democratization. Its significance in Comparative Politics is not in doubt. Because culture has local roots, it sets the tone for not only how citizens interact with each other but also how political leaders govern. The consequences of ignoring the local roots of governance have shown up in recent decades as Western governments have sponsored economic and political reforms without attention to norms and values that underlie institutions (Andrews 2013). The imperious nature of these donor-funded ventures has led to setbacks, democratic backsliding being one manifestation. It must be recognized, therefore, that culture is a slow-moving variable. Political scientists overlook this at their own cost. The more recent definition and use of political culture as communicative action is a step in the right direction because it recognizes its origin in social interaction and the possibility of changing it by democratic means. The public sphere becomes a platform for voicing alternative views to those of politicians and administrators and thus a place where issues can be developed with citizen inputs. At the same time, it must be recognized that in countries with a community-based form of politics, the space for developing a public sphere is quite limited. It is important that international non-governmental organizations involved in civic advancement projects realize that modernizing African society and making it more cosmopolitan are fraught with challenges and potential for missteps.

# 8    Four Neighbours, Four Regimes

## 8.1    INTRODUCTION

One of the striking features of African politics is the noticeable variation that exists among countries. As discussed in Chapter 5, their
embrace of democratic norms and values differs significantly from
country to country. The lack of a democratic role model in the region
is an indication that political leaders are generally preoccupied with
pursuing their own governance priorities. The important thing that
the democratization literature misses is that African leaders are not
merely at the receiving end of regime formation. They are themselves in the middle of shaping it. The fact that they differ in their
pursuit is an acknowledgment that they consider local conditions. In
the post-colonial context, their ambition is to anchor the regime in
local soil, reflecting values that circulate in society and are part of the
political discourse. This amounts, among other things, to reinventing pre-colonial values in modern contexts – Julius Nyerere's *ujamaa* version of communalism being the most well known. Doing so,
however, is fraught with difficulties stemming from the challenges of
building and managing the state-nation. It should be no surprise that
countries vary in their post-independence outlook and performance.

   This chapter recounts the political experience of four countries
in East Africa that are neighbours with a similar colonial experience.
They also have in common a legacy of generous foreign aid from
Western governments. Despite these significant commonalities,
the countries have developed quite differently since independence.
As demonstrated in Chapter 5, the East African sub-region does not
score high on democracy indicators and none of the countries stands

Table 8.1 *The four East African countries by regime type*

| Regime | Country |
| --- | --- |
| Clientelist-competitive | Kenya |
| Monopolist-movemental | Tanzania |
| Neo-patrimonial-fractured | Uganda |
| Authoritarian-modernizing | Rwanda |

*Source:* Author

out as a top performer. They are building the post-colonial state-nation in ways that reflect the respective political reality that they inherited from the colonial powers rather than trying to imitate the model that the Western donors prefer and preach. As indicated in Table 8.1, the four countries are embarked on four separate political development paths that largely correspond to the regime types identified in Chapter 5.

African leaders are caught in a governance dilemma that is more pronounced than elsewhere because of the role that the colonial legacy plays. It is not only politically expedient but also a virtual necessity in the post-colonial context that leaders demonstrate aversion to what their society inherited from the former rulers. At the same time, they must provide a convincing view of the road ahead. Leaders have a choice between two options: seeking inspiration from values dating back to pre-colonial times or imitating the path to modernity adopted by other regions in the world. Most leaders desire it would be possible to combine the two and govern accordingly. Both options, however, come with their own costs: reinforcing the institutional foundation of pre-agrarian society, for example, by perpetuating small peasant agriculture and accepting existing communities of consumption, may placate supporters but leave society with limited capacity to transform itself. Likewise, adopting ambitious modernization strategies, often to satisfy foreign donors, carries its own costs by leaving behind largely unsuccessful outcomes. This chapter will discuss how the leaders of the four East African countries have chosen their respective governance strategy in which both the past and the present matter.

## 8.2    HOW THE PAST MATTERS

When the colonial borders were drawn up in East Africa, each territory brought together ethnic groups with little regard to their past. How these local entities were constituted and how they were ruled differed. Some were pre-agrarian chiefdoms or kingdoms in which a certain social stratification existed through favours dispensed by the ruler. As argued in previous chapters, this stratification was rooted in consumption rather than production. The aristocracy or favoured caste was not a class of landlords controlling production. Instead, their status was attributable to their ability to secure favours that others were denied. Other societies were stateless or what anthropologists call "acephalous". These are groups in which elders representing lineages or clans would lead their own units and coordinate with others primarily in the case of an external threat caused by invasion of strangers or natural disasters. These pre-colonial legacies have been especially pronounced in former British colonies, as argued by Chlouba et al. (2021). In East Africa, Kenya was primarily made up of stateless groups competing for land in an open frontier; Rwanda was an old kingdom that was left by the Germans as its own colony; and Tanzania and Uganda were made up of a more complex mixture of both kingdoms and stateless groups. The respective pre-colonial past of the four countries is briefly discussed here to highlight how it matters to this day.

### 8.2.1    Kenya

In the savanna highlands of what is today Kenya, societies were ruled by clan elders and lacked a supreme leader, that is, a chief or king. These were stateless societies, which meant that they also lacked fixed boundaries. The Kikuyu, Masai, and other groups that occupied this land were frontier people who moved freely on to new lands (Kopytoff 1989). They had to get along by using reciprocal exchanges to avoid conflict, including the right to take revenge in case of attack. Kenya's politics today reflects this pre-colonial past. The British decision to alienate land to white settlers in the fertile highlands occupied primarily by the Kikuyu people obviously limited their territory and this decision eventually led to the Mau Mau uprising. Although the Kikuyus have tried to claim supremacy based on their leading role in the struggle for independence (Rabinowitz 2020), the political playing field in Kenya is relatively even, leading to intense competition between the various acephalous ethnic communities and the need for political actors to create coalitions across ethnic lines. Leading figures in each community become the focus of clientelist networks. Being able to deliver goods to their followers becomes the key to success and a sustained political career. Once a leader has a strong following, he (or she) cannot be ignored in the national conversation about who should be in government. It is among these political "patrons" that national leaders emerge. On surface, Kenyan politics appears volatile but the rules – whether formal or informal – are well known and respected by the politicians. Kenya is a perfect example of transactional politics that Berman (1998) refers to as "uncivil nationalism". Because there is no single community or party strong enough to govern on its own, it becomes hard to institutionalize an autocratic form of rule. Although there are authoritarian tendencies in Kenya society, attempts to govern in an autocratic fashion by the country's first two presidents, Jomo Kenyatta and Daniel arap Moi, were held back by the necessity to build ethnic coalitions. This tension between a vertical and a lateral use of power has continued to this day and becomes especially evident at times of election (Atieno-Odhiambo 2002; Long et al. 2013).

## 8.2.2  Rwanda

In terms of pre-colonial legacy, Rwanda is the opposite to Kenya. Borders matter and they have remained pretty much the same as they were before 1884, the year the colonizing powers in Europe agreed upon their own boundaries for Africa. It is a traditional kingdom that through violence has modernized within its own shell. The monarchy was abolished following the 1959 social revolution by the majority Hutu population, and many members of the minority ruling Tutsi aristocracy fled to neighbouring countries (Lemarchand 1970; Newbury 1988). The Hutu leaders who took over the government adopted their own logic of oppression against the minority Tutsi that culminated in the 1994 genocide. The intensification of the tensions between the two groups is attributed by leading scholars, such as Prunier (1995) and Mamdani (2001), to the Belgian colonial policy that treated the Tutsi as racially superior to the Hutus. It created a no-win situation in which the Hutus felt deprived of opportunity and the minority Tutsi feared for their own security.

After members of the Tutsi aristocracy returned from exile and seized power in 1994, the official policy has been to discourage ethnic identities in favour of a patriotic call that "we are all Rwandans". Given the legacy of conflict, it has not been easy to achieve this goal, but it is interesting that the government under President Paul Kagame has tried to ground this strategy in a reinvention of the country's pre-colonial past. Examples abound of "home-grown initiatives", such as policies that build on indigenous institutions. These include, for example, *imihigo* – a form of performance contract adapted from pre-colonial governance practices, *gacaca* courts – local platforms for civil dispute resolution, and *umuganda* – an indigenous term for communal work that has been revived to organize local development efforts (Booth and Golooba-Mutebi 2012; Huggins 2017).

Rwanda is one of the few countries in Africa that resemble the nation-state: a confluence between nationality and state, a single language and a caste-like social stratification. Rwanda's model is the East Asian developmental state. It has its own strategy of development – Vision 2050 – adopted after a broad consultation with Rwandans of all backgrounds. Participation in the Rwandan developmental state is compulsory and portrayed as a civic duty (Hasselskog and Schierenbeck 2015). While horizontal transactions are what keeps Kenya going, Rwanda relies almost exclusively on hierarchically organized transactions. Emphasis on participation in national development has become a way of promoting national unity.

### 8.2.3 Uganda

Uganda has much in common with Rwanda, but it is also different. Like so much of the land around the Great Lakes of Africa a big share of Ugandan territory is planted with bananas – a perennial crop that led to sedentary living and the growth of more complex systems of government long before the colonial powers arrived (Fallers 1956). The British, who were given control of Uganda in 1884, brought together no less than five kingdoms – Buganda, Ankole, Busoga, Bunyoro, and Toro – for which borders mattered. Disputes between especially Bunyoro and Buganda became politically heated events during colonial times and occupied much attention of the British overlords. Although they had relied on all kingdoms to participate in their administration under a system of indirect rule, Buganda became especially important because the country's capital, Kampala, is situated within its borders. As the British were withdrawing from Uganda and prepared for independence, they gave into the demand from Buganda leaders to render the kingdom a federal status within the Republic of Uganda. Furthermore, the Buganda king – the *Kabaka* – became the republic's first president. Others saw these arrangements as the creation of a "state within the state", and once the pre-independence elections had been held, the majority political party, the Uganda People's Congress, felt hampered by the favoured status of Buganda. Milton Obote – the prime minister – representing the acephalous northern region of Uganda went as far as asking the national army in 1966 to intervene by attacking the presidential palace – likewise the traditional residence of the king. The latter was forced into exile, but an equally important indirect consequence of this intervention was Field Marshal Idi Amin's coup in 1971. He had smelled the sweetness of power leading the army attack against the *Kabaka*, and five years later, he did not hesitate to overthrow Obote when the latter attended a British

Commonwealth meeting in Singapore. Uganda has remained a socially and politically fractured country in which the powers of the traditional kingdoms have remained despite attempts to lessen their influence by breaking them down into administrative districts (Hansen and Twaddle 1998).

### 8.2.4 *Tanzania*

Tanzania is a complex mixture of sedentary and nomadic peoples, none of which were really a dominant force prior to 1884 when the Germans were given the go-ahead to occupy Tanganyika, the mainland portion of what is today Tanzania (Zanzibar, under British protection at the time, being the other). Unlike Rwanda and Uganda, there was no dominant kingdom (Maddox et al. 1996). Those chiefdoms that existed, for example, in north-western Tanzania, were never influential beyond very limited territory. During colonial time there were isolated rebellions against the overlords (especially during the German occupation) but they never crystallized into a major nationalist movement. The transition to independence in Tanganyika, therefore, was peaceful. Violence would occur only after independence when the African population in Zanzibar rebelled against the ruling Arab minority. The most significant factor in the country's pre-colonial history is the legacy of the extensive slave trade that was organized by the Arabs in Zanzibar. It helped spread a common language – Swahili – that blended Arab and Bantu grammar, syntax, and vocabulary. It was first spoken in the Swahili city-states along the coast of the Indian Ocean but thanks to the trade in slaves and ivory it spread to the interior of the continent (Sheriff 1987). The country's first president, Julius Nyerere, saw the potential for national unification by making Swahili not only a lingua franca but also an official language to be used in government. The pre-colonial past, therefore, has played itself out such that Tanzania today lays claim to being a state-nation inspired by Pan-African ideals and forged together in Bantu soils. Its outlook on the world is very much determined by this process (Ibhawoh and Dibua 2003).

## 8.3 HOW THEY GOVERN

As noted in previous chapters, political scientists with an interest in how institutions shape political regimes have shown that the emergence of a bourgeoisie or middle class is a facilitator of democracy (Lipset 1959; Moore Jr 1966; Przeworski et al. 2000). Apart from training civil servants to become the elite of the new states, the colonial powers did little to foster an indigenous middle class. To this day, the middle class is weak and lacks the autonomy to use the state as a driver of change. There are differences, however, in terms of the level of development. Kenya has reached "middle-income" status while the other three are still trying to get there. According to World Development data, the latter were growing the fastest in 2019, the last year before the Covid-19 pandemic set in, but the level of economic development in Kenya remains considerably higher than in the other three countries. These figures, as suggested in Table 8.2, also suggest that at this low level of per capita income, the scope for the growth of a strong middle class is limited.

The sociological use of "middle class" usually refers to a group of people (1) with money to spare for a way of life beyond spending it all on daily living and (2) with a common interest in moving society forward (Lopez and Weinstein 2012). The middle class is likely to develop in tandem with the growth and diversification of the national economy. That is one reason why the middle class in African countries is generally quite small. In many countries, its members are

Table 8.2 *Macro-economic data per country, 2019*

| Country | GDP per capita (current PPP)* | Growth per capita (current PPP) |
|---|---|---|
| Kenya | $4,520 | 5.4% |
| Tanzania | $2,771 | 5.8% |
| Rwanda | $2,325 | 9.4% |
| Uganda | $2,284 | 6.8.% |

* PPP = Purchasing Power Parity
*Source:* World Development Report (2020)

primarily found in the public sector constrained by bureaucracy when wishing to be innovative and entrepreneurial. Furthermore, as Shivji (1976) noted about the "bureaucratic bourgeoisie" in Tanzania, it is not productive. Although he uses a different terminology, his analysis confirms the presence of a politics grounded in consumption communities rather than social classes tied to the means of production. The middle class, therefore, is still to fully emerge in African society to play its role as a pioneer of development as it has in other regions of the world. Recent macro-economic data, as presented in Table 8.2, confirms the relatively low level of economic development in the sub-region.

The middle class in Kenya comes the closest to being autonomous and diverse enough to drive a process of modernization. The result is that the country is taking on features of modernity typically associated with developed countries. With Nairobi serving as the regional hub, Kenya has many advantages, and the emerging local middle class has not hesitated to grab them. Its members are influential not only in professional and business circles but also in the growing voluntary sector. Rwanda is doing its best to accelerate the emergence of a local middle class without losing its sense of direction as a developmental state. The result is a corporate society where opportunities for individual advancement exist but only within a tightly controlled system (Crisafulli and Redmond 2014). Tanzania and Uganda are more ambivalent about the role of the middle class. In Tanzania, for example, the official strategy under the founding president, Julius Nyerere, and more lately under President John Magufuli,[1] has been to hold back its growth, initially through nationalization of private property and later by heavy taxation. Uganda, finally, may not officially be as suspicious of foreign investors as Tanzania, but even there, members of the local middle class operate under a cloud of political capriciousness that hampers its growth (Blanshe 2021).

---

[1] President Magufuli died in 2021 after having served from 2015. He was succeeded by his vice-president, Samia Suluhu-Hassan.

With these distinguishing features of the pre-colonial past and post-independence present in mind, the question is, what difference do the emerging regimes make for how countries are governed? To get a sense of it, the chapter focuses on three areas of governance: (1) integrity of public office, (2) local governance, and (3) business climate. They cover key economic and political dimensions of how the state functions as well as its relation to society.

Each of the three areas will reveal something important about how countries are governed. The sub-section on the integrity of public office discusses the strength of formal institutions but also how informal ones operate inside the state. The one on local governance is significant because it indicates the confidence government leaders have in sharing power with locally elected politicians and overcoming the strong central control of government that evolved at independence. The discussion of how government approaches business indicates its level of trust in the private sector, including foreign investors. This issue has become increasingly important as African countries have become of great interest to investors.

## 8.3.1   Public Integrity

Violation of the principle of integrity of public office is one of the most common features of African governance. As communities of consumption compete within a limited access order, it is no surprise that large amounts of public money are diverted into alternative uses. For example, even though the size of illicit outflows from African countries is hard to know, according to one report compiled by UK and African development activists, in 2015 it may have amounted to US$40 billion more than what the continent received in aid, loans, and personal remittances (*The Guardian*, London, 11 May 2016). Corruption engenders widespread suspicion and criticism from citizens across the continent. In its Round 6 (2014–15), the Afrobarometer found that 72 per cent of Africans see at least "some" officials in their country's presidency as corrupt, including 31 per cent who say that all officials in that office are corrupt. Perceptions of corruption are even higher when it comes to members of parliament, local government councillors, tax officials, judges, and police (Frinjuah and Appiah-Nyamekye 2018). There is reason, however, to be circumspect when interpreting these figures for African countries. In societies organized into competing communities of consumption, criticism of corruption often entails just a bemoaning that it does not benefit oneself and one's own community. The Ghanaian saying that "it is our time to chop" reminds us about the extent to which public office is a source of extracting resources rather than protecting public goods. Against this background, the question is, how well are the four East African countries handling this issue?

The standard source for measuring corruption is based on the perception of it – the closest one can come to get a sense of its role in public life. Transparency International provides a score for each country and then ranks it on a global list of countries. According to its 2020 report, Rwanda scored considerably higher than its East African neighbours (54 on a scale of 100, with Tanzania scoring 38, Uganda 31, and Kenya 27). In global ranking, Rwanda came in at number 49, with the others trailing: Tanzania 94, Uganda 124, and Kenya 142 (Transparency International 2020). Although the East African countries, regardless of regime, have a long way to go to wipe out corruption, only the highly disciplinary but also autocratic regime of President Kagame in Rwanda, whom *The Economist* (15 July 2017) has referred to as "the hard man of the hills", can compete with the best African performers – Botswana and Cape Verde. The details for the four East African countries are provided in Table 8.3.

Perhaps the most interesting thing about these figures is the relatively high score of Tanzania, which can be attributed to the work of President Magufuli to combat corruption during his time in office (2015–21). Even if his methods were questionable from a human rights perspective, he earned the support of Tanzanians as confirmed in a study based on Afrobarometer data (Olan'g and Msami 2018). That Kenya places last should be no surprise. It reflects the relatively cosmopolitan outlook of its urban citizens, notably among members of

Table 8.3 *Perceived corruption levels in East Africa*

| Country | Score | Rank |
| --- | --- | --- |
| Rwanda | 54 | 49 |
| Tanzania | 38 | 94 |
| Uganda | 31 | 124 |
| Kenya | 27 | 142 |

*Source:* Transparency International (2020)

the strong Christian faith communities. Both awareness and abhorrence of corruption help explain this finding. President Kenyatta initiated a public campaign in 2018 proclaiming that he wants to make the anti-corruption campaign part of his presidential legacy. This tremendously complex task goes beyond what the president can do on his own but other branches of government have been activated to participate in the campaign. For example, following the president's announcement, Kenya's public prosecutor initiated cases against some well-heeled individuals, notably those who had constructed private buildings on public land (*The Standard*, Nairobi, 14 August 2018).

President Museveni initiated his own anti-corruption campaign in 2006, and it was followed up with a solid administrative and legal framework that was widely praised by the international donor community. Corruption, however, has persisted and the country's ranking on the global Corruption Prevention Index (CPI) has fallen. Widespread complaints among Ugandans resulted in an admission by the president in 2018 that he must start all over again (*AfricaNews*, 18 September 2018). Very much in line with how presidents in Africa operate, he provided the Ugandan public with a local "800" number, which he claimed he had set up in his office so members of the public could call him directly if they encounter cases of corruption. Because corruption in African countries is an expression of their structural set-up as communities of consumption and not merely an example of deviant behaviour as the case tends to be in developed societies, calling the president's special number may not be a waste but experience suggests that the likelihood that it affects the level of corruption in the country is not great (Gwen 2011).

### 8.3.2    Local Governance

Local governance was a cornerstone in the British scheme to prepare their colonies for independence. They saw local governments as schools of governance where officials could be tutored to adopt good practices. They believed that involving Africans at the local level was an essential step towards building a system of democratic governance. Many post-independence leaders benefitted from this training. The French and the Belgians paid less attention to this aspect of the decolonization process. Elected local government structures have never played as prominent a role in their former colonies as they have where the British served as overlords.

The autonomy of local governments, however, did not last long after independence. Tanzania went furthest by abolishing its local government system and replacing it with a centrally controlled administrative system justified as a means of making development efforts more effective. A similar but less drastic approach was adopted in Kenya where a Rural Development Strategy became the justification for rendering the country's county councils less independent. Decentralization was also eventually curbed in the post-independence period in Uganda, but it was a more complicated and contentious process because of the power of the Buganda Kingdom and its own local governance structure. Gradually, however, the autonomy of local government institutions was curtailed, and power concentrated in the central government, a process that was formalized in the 1967 constitution and culminated during Amin's rule in the 1970s. In Rwanda, elite vulnerability played a large part in keeping power centralized in the early post-colonial period.

Decentralization in the form of devolution of power to local government authorities has proved difficult to accept for African government leaders, but a bold and concerted effort has been made in Kenya where devolution to local counties is a reality since the

2010 Constitution was adopted. Not only are these entities able to raise their own revenue, but they are also guaranteed a specified minimum share of the national budget. This has proved to be a game changer because political power is now more evenly distributed between the centre and the periphery. Elected political positions such as governor and senator at the county level have acquired prestige and are viewed as attractive as becoming a high-level government official such as cabinet or permanent secretary. The Kenyan devolution project is still in a settling-in phase but there are no signs that political leaders want to abandon it. On the contrary, their minds are set to improve and institutionalize it. Such was the mood at the Fifth Annual Devolution Conference in April 2018, which brought together stakeholders at all levels for a joint assessment. As the Opposition leader, Raila Odinga, stressed, graft poses the most serious threat to devolution, but there was also unanimity in the decision to work towards eliminating corruption (*Daily Nation*, Nairobi, 28 April 2018).

Its neighbours have followed different paths. The Tanzanian government has concentrated revenue collection in the hands of its Revenue Authority. Municipal and district councils that previously could collect their own revenue and thus be assured of recurrent income to provide services, notably maintenance of roads and other infrastructure, must now beg on their knees to get a share, generally much less than what they need, from central government. Local government authorities in Tanzania also fall short of their objectives because they cannot afford to hire enough employees, as reported by the National Audit Office in May 2018 (*The Citizen*, Dar es Salaam, 3 May 2018).

Decentralization became a buzzword in Uganda after the National Resistance Movement had taken power in 1986. The resistance councils that were set up by Museveni and his lieutenants as they liberated the country from the grip of Amin became the foundation for a new system of bottom-up governance. While this system has strengthened public accountability at grassroots level, it has fallen short of devolving real power. The local-level organs have not been given the revenue collection power that would make devolution a reality in the country (Francis and James 2003).

Rwanda adopted its own decentralization in 2000 but focusing on results rather than the process. Its policy is explicitly to ensure equitable social, political, and economic development. The policy refers also to strengthening citizen participation but on terms set by the government (Hasselskog and Schierenbeck 2015). This means that citizen participation amounts to following orders from above, often conveyed in technical language (Huggins 2017).

The story of local governance in the region, therefore, is varied. The four regimes have followed their own distinct paths, with Kenya clearly having gone the furthest in devolution while the other three have held on to various degrees of centralized rule. This is the case especially in Rwanda, although it can also display positive results from its "citizen mobilization" strategy. The discrepancy between promise and practice is apparent in Tanzania and Uganda. Both have local-level institutions, but neither possesses the right to collect and retain revenue on their own. The dominance of the ruling party in Tanzania makes it possible to allocate resources according to party loyalty while a fairer, albeit discretionary, distribution takes place in Uganda where buying loyalty is still a necessary part of the country's transactional governance.

### 8.3.3   Business Climate

The role of the private sector in national development has become increasingly important, fostered to a large extent by globalization. After having largely been avoided by foreign investors for a long time, African countries have more recently become destinations of investment. Many of these investments have been made with the view of extracting resources from the continent, but whatever the motive African countries cannot escape the new interest that outside investors show. The question is, how do these countries relate to it and how do they handle business? Do they provide a hospitable or hostile climate? The four East African countries, once again, display their differences.

In 2018, Rwanda and Kenya were responding with a welcome, while Tanzania and to a lesser extent Uganda were hesitant, if not outright hostile, in welcoming foreign investors. Because both countries possess oil and gas resources, they know that they can strike a good bargain with any business organization to get access. This is especially true for Tanzania where the revival of the spectre of a state-led development has led to uneasiness among Tanzanian as well as foreign members of the business community. President Magufuli's populist rhetoric portrayed ordinary Tanzanians as victims of exploitation by private companies. Now that he is no longer around, things seem to change, and the current president, Samia Suluhu Hassan, has signalled commitment to a more business-friendly environment.

The situation in Uganda is different in that much of it has centred on the role of Asian business owners whose parents or grandparents were forced to leave in 1972 when Amin launched his campaign against the Asian-Ugandan community. Since President Museveni came to power in the mid-1980s, members of this community have been able to reclaim their lost property and many of them are now among the biggest investors in Uganda (Portes et al. 2020).

Kenya has always been open for business and it is still the main destination for outside investors in the region. In addition, the indigenous private sector has had time to establish itself as a force of its own, offering the prospect of attractive partnerships for foreign investors. Rwanda is not following Kenya in all respects, but in encouraging business, it does so. The government realizes the value of combining a state-led strategy with carrots for both local and foreign investors. This sets it aside from Tanzania, which is the other country in the region where the state is placed in the position of a principal driver of change.

These differences show up in statistics about how easy it is to establish a business in the region. Table 8.4 indicates the position that the four countries occupy in the global ranking of "ease of doing business" as well as their position on specific aspects of doing so.

Table 8.4 *Ease of doing business in East Africa, by country*

| Country | Global rank | Start business | Get permits | Get electricity | Register property | Get credit | Protection of minority investors |
|---------|-------------|----------------|-------------|-----------------|-------------------|------------|-----------------------------------|
| Rwanda | 29 | 51 | 106 | 68 | 2 | 3 | 14 |
| Kenya | 51 | 126 | 128 | 75 | 122 | 8 | 11 |
| Uganda | 127 | 163 | 145 | 175 | 126 | 73 | 110 |
| Tanzania | 144 | 164 | 150 | 83 | 146 | 60 | 131 |

*Source:* World Development Data (2020)

The scores of the four countries are generally highest on the banking side. Getting credit is especially easy in Kenya and Rwanda. These two also score significantly higher on the protection of minority investors, confirming that both countries value partnership with foreigners. Rwanda is alone at the top when it comes to registering property, a process that in the other countries is time-consuming and often involves paying bribes. Corruption also features in getting permits for construction. Out of the total 190 countries included in the ease of doing business survey, none of the East African countries appears in the upper half of the list. Nor does any of them register a top score on getting electricity, with Uganda trailing the other three by a wide margin. In a wider comparative perspective, the four East African countries are not competitive in enabling the process of starting a business. Yet within the region there is variation that reflects the different modes by which they are being governed.

## 8.4 CONCLUSIONS

This analysis of the four countries confirms the evolution of variable patterns of governance based on how they approach the issues of managing the state-nation. Each country has chosen its own development path and built a political system around the local challenges of transcending the structural limits inherent in their pre-agrarian society. The result is that governments tend to look inwards in their approach to what needs to be done and, as in the case of Tanzania, on and off engage in Marxian critique of development ideas originating in the West (Nursey-Bray 1980; Blommaert 2013). This is an indication of how several African governments think and respond to the challenges of social transformation inherent in the modernization of society. Any attempt at making rapid forward progress easily rattles the social order, a threat that is especially imminent in the process of shifting from a social formation based on consumption communities to one founded in the economic production process. The genocide in Rwanda in 1994 is an example of how this process may go awry. So are the incidents of ethnic strife that have afflicted Kenya. Yet, the process of overcoming the structural limitations of a pre-agrarian society is integral to the issues examined in this chapter: strengthening public integrity, devolving political authority, and promoting business.

# 9 What Africa Teaches Us

Political scientists strive to be "real" scientists. This ambition to imitate the natural sciences, however, has its limitations. As this book has tried to demonstrate, such is the case in the study of Comparative Politics. The subject matter is not inanimate. Politics has its own dynamic that is not really captured once and for all in a single theory. Instead, theories come and go. Comparativists cannot sit back and enjoy more than a moment of "normal science". Their search for fresh knowledge is open-ended and as reliant on new theoretical insights as they are on already established theory. We cannot stop the world, nor can we jump off to do our analysis in splendid isolation. Temptation to do so, however, has increased with the availability of standardized metadata sets. The result is that reality features less in comparative analysis and is overshadowed by a fictitious version that passes as authoritative. It is in this context that regions and countries of the world that are structurally and culturally different from the mainstream Western model of politics lose their position as entities of interest. The possible alternative of trying to make politics in Africa or Asia the basis for comparing other regions would be a non-starter because it goes up against established thinking and powers in the discipline.

This book reluctantly acknowledges this reality of the field and uses Africa as an example to highlight the limits of comparisons based on theories derived from the political experience of already developed and democratic societies. Democracy has been taken for granted as best illustrated in the phrase "the only game in town".

Comparative Politics has been turned almost exclusively into comparative democratization – at the expense of attention to how and why countries change. This final chapter is meant to highlight the many significant omissions that follow from relying primarily on a democratic theory lens. African politics, like that of other developing and democratizing regions, is much more complex. Above all, the social forces that drive it are foremost local. The interesting issue, therefore, is not how well the countries score on a global democracy scale but how existing structures accommodate the presence of democratic values and norms.

## 9.2 RELEVANCE OF AN AFRICANIST PERSPECTIVE

The experience that Africa and these other regions have in "living with democracy" is becoming increasingly central to Comparative Politics as ongoing global demographic and economic changes generate new forms of politics in Europe and North America. Social cleavages based on identity are getting more common and pronounced in countries where they had once been modified if not neutralized by modernization and the growth of social class divisions. As discussed in Chapter 4, nation-states are increasingly becoming state-nations where managing heterogeneity overshadows sustaining homogeneity. Globalization has upset the social landscape in significant ways causing new anxieties and fears, such as of minority religions and immigrant groups. This increasingly common form of politics across regions of the world is shifting positive-sum into zero-sum games and threatening the civic norms on which democratic effectiveness and legitimacy rest. Globalization, as suggested earlier, is also upsetting the relative stability of political party systems as voters abandon those that were built on the once prevailing social class divisions and instead embrace populist parties in which strong personalities rather than enlightened choice settle disputes. When viewing current political tendencies in Europe and the Americas from an Africanist perspective, it is hard not to notice the similarities with features that have been dominant in African politics for a long time.

There are reasons, therefore, why comparative political analysis needs to move on beyond theoretical constructs that only capture the moral battles between autocracy and democracy. Backsliding of democratic norms and institutions are painful to watch for the enlightened Westerner who experiences the fate of democracy as an existential issue of life and death. This disposition, however, which is evident in the dominant theorizing on democracy, limits the scope and orientation of comparative research. Democracy needs to be explained, not be taken for granted. Highlighting the local context in which democracy functions provides a more insightful and realistic perspective on the prospects for its development.

This conclusion is organized to bring together the issues discussed in previous chapters. In so doing, it reviews (1) what the focus on Africa has revealed, (2) how global forces change the terms of comparative political analysis, and (3) and how the next generation of comparativists might approach theorizing about politics.

## 9.3   WHAT AFRICA HAS REVEALED

In discussing Africa's dual status as a region with its own special features while also being increasingly integrated with the rest of the world, the account in this book has highlighted six points that are of interest for further consideration in Comparative Politics theorizing: (1) context matters, (2) history is local, (3) state development varies, (4) regimes are in the making, (5) institutions are not objective, and (6) parties function without ideology. These are observations that have applications in other parts of the world. They will be further elaborated here.

### 9.3.1   Context Matters

This general point is important to guide future thinking about the evolution of Comparative Politics. The idea that the Western experience can serve as a starting point for comparison leads to several shortcomings that this review of the field from an African perspective has revealed. One is the teleological logic that is built into such a design. It assumes a given model of development that other countries are presumed to follow because of its moral superiority. The West becomes both the end-station and the guidepost to get there. Although there is a rich political history of the West and the pain and joy associated with it, this record is left out of the theorizing that has guided comparative analysis since the emergence of interest in democratization over thirty years ago. The result is that the analysis has become free of context and focused almost exclusively on measuring the normative quality of democratic institutions. This has produced a second shortcoming: evaluation of performance in relation to a theoretical model rather than in relation to changes in local conditions. The literature is short on accounts of what it means for countries to democratize. How the West got there is conveniently overlooked in favour of a moralist interpretation of the role that democracy plays as a positive force for both governance and development. Such an approach is too thin. The African case, discussed here, highlights this.

## 9.3.2 History Is Local

History in Comparative Politics typically enters theorizing as Big History. Some very influential pieces discussed in this book have deliberated the role that revolutions and wars have played in shaping states and regimes. Again, it is the European experience that has been in the forefront although big countries elsewhere like China, India, and Japan have also been covered. Less dramatic turns in history, however, become equally important if the analysis drills down to the specifics of other countries and regions. This book has shown its significant role in ex-colonial settings where nationalist leaders are anxious to rid their countries of the colonial legacy while at the same time reinvent their pre-colonial past as a guide to the future. As noted in Chapter 5, in most African countries this act has been conducted peacefully although there are also cases where political development since independence has been conflictual. One example is where leaders went as far as cutting virtually all ties with their former masters. Another is where leaders pulled in the opposite direction and used their power to create nativist scenarios that privileged some ethnic groups over others as in Cameroon and the Ivory Coast. This latter tendency is by no means confined to Africa and has emerged in the Americas, Europe, and some Asian countries like India and Myanmar. The historical dimension of contemporary politics, therefore, is an essential ingredient that can only be ignored at the cost of a thin and incomplete account. "Work with the Grain", Levy (2014) exhorts development practitioners and points to the local roots of development. The message is relevant also for those of us who theorize about the subject.

### 9.3.3   State Development Varies

The nation-state as it came into existence in Europe in the nineteenth and early twentieth centuries has been the standard reference point in most comparative studies of the state, but the concept has lost much of its place in more recent comparative political analysis. It has played virtually no role in the literature on democratization. Uneven political development, therefore, has been explained by other factors, notably institutions. A focus on Africa underlines the importance of research on both statehood and statecraft. Countries in the region are in the middle of forming the nation through state action. Although all nation-states were originally formed by state action, once the issue is settled, interest in how the nation-state first came about tends to vanish. Such is not the case in African countries where states in the post-colonial context are still busily engaged in building the nation. As this book has argued, no other objective is more important than building the political community into a more cohesive entity. The same focus is emerging in many other countries around the world but often for reasons related to accommodating new immigrants. The slumbering nation-state is being shaken into action and is becoming more pro-active like its African counterpart. The African experience, therefore, is taking centre stage in efforts to theorize state development. The variety of such development around the world is certainly becoming more evident and of greater interest than before, especially since it tends to affect the quality of governance.

### 9.3.4   Regimes in the Making

The literature on comparative democratization has not been interested in how regimes come about and provide differential degrees of space for democratic development. Its focus instead has been on what happens when democratic norms and institutions are being transferred to countries without a democratic tradition. The omission in the analysis of structural realities and domestic institutional legacies has generated narratives that are thick on democracy conceptualization but thin on country comprehension. In fact, the concept has become the end rather than the means of doing comparative political analysis. The emphasis on creating ladders grounded in the normative qualities of Western democracy reduces Comparative Politics to an evaluative enterprise. The field needs to adopt an approach that focuses on the factual conditions that exist in countries where political actors are still preoccupied with forming legitimate institutional arrangements. Variable regime patterns have their roots in factors that go beyond their level of democracy. Without a full understanding of these contextual factors, quantitative data on democracy are of limited value.

### 9.3.5   Institutions More than Formal Rules

The standard conception of institutions in the field stipulates that they are the rules that guide moral and political behaviour and choice. The overarching rules are typically enacted by politically elected representatives of the people. Rules are treated as existing independently of human will. The rule of law prevails, and the individual citizen is not expected to take the law into his own hands. Institutions may be changed but only through a formal decision process. Changing meta-institutions like constitutions typically involve several layers of approval before it can be enacted. Treating institutions this way, however, misses the informality with which

politics is conducted – often successfully. The Swedish democratization process is a case in point. It occurred over a hundred-year
period against the background of a monarchic and non-democratic
constitution adopted in 1809. Democracy evolved peacefully in an
informal and incremental manner without attempts to change the
basic law. The process was completed in the first half of the twentieth century but a new constitution officially revoking the 1809 version was not adopted until 1974. This suggests that institutions are
not independent of human habits but are, as suggested in the earlier
review, part and parcel of how individuals think and act. This point
is relevant in the many countries where leaders are in the process of
building regimes for their country. Their own experience and leadership become decisive in "setting the tone" for how politics is being
conducted. Institutions, therefore, change in the context of human
practice. This book has illustrated how regimes that are still in the
making in African countries depend on informal relations to lay the
foundation for stability amidst the challenges associated with managing the state-nation.

### 9.3.6   Parties without Ideology

The standard notion of political parties in Comparative Politics is that
they are organizations driven by a specific ideology typically rooted
in economic interests. Ever since the 1950s and especially after the
overview of political parties in Europe by Lipset and Rokkan (1967),
political parties have been identified along a left–right spectrum. The
European party scene has changed more recently as new parties have
emerged to compete with the "traditional" ones. Especially significant has been the rise of "green" parties, that is, those that build their
support by appealing to the need for environmental protection and
management as well as concern about climate change. Even so, ideology is what defines political parties. In many countries in the developing world, however, ideology does not have such a prominent role.
The main reason is that modernization is yet to produce the conflict
between capital and labour that is the basis for parties in developed

countries. Thus, political parties are functioning in a more pragmatic manner where personal leadership and strategic social interactions dominate. Even if ideology was an inspiration in the struggle for independence, it has not been a significant feature of African politics in the post-colonial context. Every attempt to resurrect the ideological drives of the past has quickly lost its draw and ability to mobilize people. In the absence of defining ideological differences, policy programmes are generally those that respond to outside donor interest or demand. This means that policy positions among political parties in Africa tend to be defined by their country's external relations, especially those with their foreign donors.

## 9.4  THE NEW CHALLENGES

Africa is a major illustration of what theorizing in Comparative Politics in the last three decades has left by the wayside. As such, it is a marker for rethinking comparative analysis in a context where assessing degrees of democracy or autocracy is becoming less and less productive. Scholars such as Rich (2017) and Levitsky and Ziblatt (2018) refer to the crisis in democracy as an institutional quandary, a position that is also held by Freedom House (2020). They point to how citizens no longer engage with political parties as they used to do and how they take their lead from a populist leader rather than specific ideological positions. While these observations are accurate and supported by research (e.g., Norris and Inglehart 2019; Revelli 2019), they do not go deep enough to identify the underlying causes of this crisis or quandary.

The crisis in democracy and the rise of populism cannot be blamed only on human nature. As a specific type of regime, democracy operates in a political system that in turn is nested in a wider social system. What matters in the analysis of democracy today is how it is being shaped or reshaped by forces that are only partially possible for political actors to control and manipulate. Public policy is one way of doing so, but politics is not autonomous of its social or economic base. It is as much a response to changes in this base

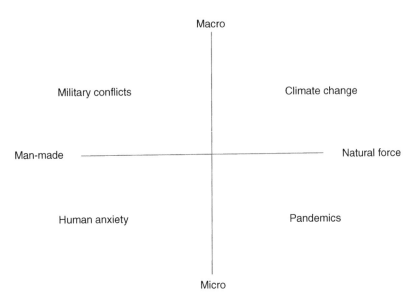

FIGURE 9.1 Global threats to liberal democracy
Source: Author

as it is an instrument or driver of change. The tendency to overlook the limits of political agency has been enforced by the global policy emphasis on ambitious but rather unrealistic development goals and targets. Freedom, justice, and inclusivity are convincing moral imperatives, but their implementation tends to lag, because not enough attention is being paid to the real conditions in which their universal dissemination is expected to take place. It is only more recently that globalization has laid bare these realities and their threat to liberal democracy in various forms.

The threats are a combination of factors, some man-made, others lying beyond human control. They manifest themselves at both macro and micro levels, as illustrated in Figure 9.1.

Military conflicts are in many respects the least "new" of the challenges because they have been a threat to political order, including liberal democracy, for many years. What is new, however, is that the cause of the conflict has changed. Secular or non-religious causes dominated during the twentieth century and have not wholly vanished as Russia's war in Ukraine indicates. Nonetheless, data on the causes of war in the last five decades indicate that conflicts based on religious identity or religious issues have increased this century (Strand et al. 2019). Identity-based conflicts involving the use of force have afflicted countries like Afghanistan, Myanmar, and the Philippines in Asia, Somalia, Mali, and the Democratic Republic of Congo in Africa, and Armenia, Iraq, and Syria in the Middle East. The severity of these conflicts has in several instances been exacerbated by the involvement of external actors with greater military power. Europe and North America have been largely spared from large-scale conflicts but violence by extremist groups, whether on the right or the left, has been on the increase. The roots of these conflicts lie in the forces of globalization that have brought people into relations with others whom they do not know and may fear. Charismatic leaders take advantage of such situations and are often behind the perpetration of communal violence. It is well known that religious communities have lived side by side in peace for generations, but when their social conditions are subject to unanticipated change, members may find the calls of a "king" appealing and consoling. In this circumstance, they easily forget that throwing themselves into his hands may in the end lead to their involuntary submission to the whims of a powerful individual interested only in his own destiny. The way white Christian evangelicals in the United States have allowed themselves to be waylaid by such a "king" – Donald J. Trump – is a vivid case in point.

The cause of climate change can be significantly attributed to human interventions, but its effects come from natural force. The global warming trend is especially alarming since it increases the threat of uncertainty under which increasing numbers of people must live. It has several deleterious consequences. As the massive icesheets that cover Greenland and Antarctica melt, sea levels will rise worldwide and threaten human habitation along low-lying coastlines, the coral islands of the Maldives in the Indian Ocean being an example where people are already forced to move to higher grounds.

Global warming also threatens major city centres like Miami and New York, potentially forcing millions of people to move. The increase in intensity of the most extreme storms that have occurred on an annual basis around the world since 1981 should be an ample warning (Reguero et al. 2019). Much of this upward trend can be attributed to warmer ocean temperatures, one that scientists deem unlikely to cease any time soon. Cyclones in Asia and the Pacific and hurricanes in Central and North America are causing not only greater physical damage but also deeper worries among people, many of whom lack the opportunity to escape the ravages of these storms.

Global warming, however, is not only about rising ocean levels and temperatures. It is also about desertification and droughts that affect agricultural cultivation in both temperate and tropical zones. Drought occurs when there are variations from normal rainfall during a season, year, or extended period of other denomination. This phenomenon is not new in many parts of the world, such as the Horn of Africa where it occurs on a regular basis, but drought conditions affect more and more people as freshwater levels fall short of what is needed for cultivation and human consumption. Such is the case, for example, in South America and Africa, where it threatens human livelihoods. There are other effects that are less directly affecting human livelihoods such as the loss of certain animal species, but regardless of its immediate consequences global warming creates conditions of doubt that affect how human beings react politically. Although the cause is global, the response is likely to be local, with a focus on "us first". International humanitarian responses may mitigate the sense of uncertainty, but being a temporary intervention, it leaves local communities in distress open to authoritarian interventions by political leaders anxious to demonstrate their role as saviour.

Like wars, pandemics are not new in a historical perspective, but what is different today is that globalization makes the spread of viruses faster and more difficult to control. In the last few decades there are at least four epidemics that have translated into cross-national pandemics: Ebola, MERS, SARS, and most recently Covid-19.

Like strong storms, the pandemics have occurred more often and caused greater number of victims. These events often have negative social and political consequences as the case was, for instance, with the 1901 plague in Cape Town, which stigmatized certain groups like Africans and Jews (because they were alleged to live in filthy conditions), thereby contributing to the foundation of the apartheid system that was institutionalized half a century later (Van Heyningen 1981; Giblin 1995). Covid-19 has caused similar forms of discrimination, especially of people of East Asian descent because the pandemic started in Wuhan, China. The presence of the pandemic has furthermore led to restrictions on movement and to a polarization of society between those who put individual freedom over human security and others who place security first. The issue of how much restriction society can take has become "weaponized" and encouraged the rise of populist leaders. This collective anxiety arising from the threat of an assertive disease is a challenge to democracy and a contributor to its backsliding. The immunity of the democratic order has its limits, a condition that has been evident in developing regions for a long time but which has shown up in recent years in Europe and North America as well.

Anxiety is also felt by individuals in their everyday interactions. The causes are many but one that seems especially serious stems from a sense of being deprived. In the United States, for example, this is true for members of the country's minority groups but also for white low-income workers who have for long taken life for granted and rarely before had to engage in politics to defend their station in life. Faced with a more diverse population these individuals are open to calls for conserving the privileges they enjoy in the status quo. Populist leaders like Trump arise in these circumstances to claim to be the voice of a "silent majority". Challenges to white Anglo-Saxon supremacy have occurred before in US history but they have grown in intensity in recent decades when new immigrants have come from developing rather than other developed countries. Populist politicians have taken advantage of these anxieties to make the white majority fearful of these new immigrants. This "we-versus-them" atmosphere has also emerged in other countries to foster the rise of a populist leadership. In Hungary, the anxiety has been turned into fear of Muslims, in Italy into fear of Africans, and in Catholic Poland into fear of secular forces.

Anxiety is systemic. It is a characteristic of our times and of our own creation. The use of science has given us many material benefits but our pursuit of a better life through the use of an instrumental or technical rationality has left many people around the world confused about the ultimate meaning of life. This is especially true in developed societies that have been largely shaped by the Enlightenment. Reason has for a long time been their empowering tool to produce economic and social development both at home and in developing countries. The multi-billion foreign aid business rests wholly on rational cost–benefit calculations that externalize anything that cannot be translated into numbers. What is being accomplished in these circumstances is meaningful only within specific project parameters. It lacks a link to human life in its wider meaning.

Only recently has it dawned on representatives of the international development community that project ownership must be localized and external support directed to work from the bottom-up, as Levy (2014) recommends. Policy or project blueprints are impersonal devices that typically do not fit the local conditions. Being pre-designed in a rational way to maximize returns, these projects and policies have little direct relationship to the livelihoods of those they are expected to benefit. For example, when donors call for evidence-based policymaking, the only evidence that counts is the one that fits into these pre-designed frames. This may be less obvious in projects conducted by international non-governmental organizations, where a participatory component is usually built into formulating and managing the activities. The problem, however, exists even in these cases because the ultimate accountability is to the board of external financing bodies. While there may be genuine efforts to develop and cultivate a communicative rationality that allows for some form of co-ownership and joint management, there is little way around technical or economic rationality for any actor with the ambition to change local society from the outside in. Going local in development practice, therefore, has its challenges.

Academics are not necessarily constrained by the same forces as policy actors, and it is their role to point out the controversies or challenges that arise when simplified theoretical frameworks are developed by these actors to suit their own goals and interests. This includes comparativists and their relation to the way democratic theory has come to uncritically dominate both research and policy. Political development is a complex process as the history of developed democracies shows. Research on democracy is incomplete without contextualization and, notably, a recognition that democracy takes time to build. Measuring the moral qualities of democracy on a global scale through institutional indicators misses these points. Such research ignores what politics is all about by underestimating the factors in society that shape politics. For these reasons, Comparative Politics will benefit from adopting a realist perspective to better appreciate what is going on around the world.

## 9.5 FROM MORALISM TO REALISM

The overwhelming emphasis on comparative democratization has generated a readiness to uncritically adopt an institutional equilibrium model derived from the historical experience of already mature democracies. This research has put the cart before the horse by focusing more on variations of democracy than variations in conditions for democratization. To reset the agenda, there is a need to identify the factors that really matter in efforts to democratize and begin theorizing accordingly. The building blocks of a new approach are (1) socioeconomic structures, (2) power dynamics, and (3) reciprocal causality.

### 9.5.1 Socio-Economic Structures

New factors are increasingly shaping politics around the world. Research on democratization may identify a causal factor, but it is merely proximate and it offers only a partial perspective on what is going on. More seriously, it ignores the contextual factors that determine the scope for democratic development. This omission is especially serious given the rise of populism and various forms of illiberal governance. This study has shown that democracy in the case of African countries is overshadowed by the complex task of managing development and holding the state-nation together. Governance in these countries is, above all, about putting in place ideologies, systems, and practices that make the state an effective instrument of securing order and promoting development. This is a task that remains unfulfilled not only in Africa but also in many countries in other developing regions. Unlike advanced societies like Sweden, where governance means managing systems already in place, governance in developing regions of the world is about making society more legible by institutionalizing effective state routines (Scott 1998). Analysts who view developing regions from the perspective of an already developed democratic society tend to overlook what it means to be "developing" and the inclination in these places to prioritize development over democracy. The latter is not an end in and of itself but one of many instruments that voters and decision-makers consider when promoting human progress. That is why the "big picture" matters.

### 9.5.2   Power Dynamics

Democracy research has treated institutions as structures of voluntary co-operation that resolve collective action problems and benefit all. This optimistic interpretation of institutions obliterates the other side of institutions: their existence as structures of power (Moe 2005). Institutions are not neutral but good for some and bad for others. They are part of a political dynamic. The liberal internationalist order is an example of how governments in low-income countries have been subjected to institutional arrangements without the ability to influence their implementation except by "voting with their feet". Donor governments have applied punitive measures such as suspending their aid to make their counterparts in developing regions go along with these rules of the game but with limited success. The liberal order has its supporters in African countries but foremost among civil society activists who find themselves excluded from influence over government policy. Donor support of civil society organizations complicates the advancement of democratic values because it often sets government against citizens in a zero-sum manner. While such confrontations may cause a breakthrough to a more pluralist order, as happened in the Arab Uprising 2011, governments are also ready to quickly retreat into authoritarianism to pre-empt threats to the social and political order. Their calculations are not necessarily based in self-interest but rather grounded in more complex judgments reflecting the broader challenges of developing a society. Comparative political analysis needs to fully consider the power dynamics that determine governance in countries across the world.

### 9.5.3   Reciprocal Causality

Although the general practice in social science analysis is to adopt a linear causation frame, there are other ways of approaching causality. Linear causality presupposes a direct link between cause and effect and has a clear beginning and a clear end. Effect can be traced back to a single cause. A more complex version of the same is the domino approach, which assumes an extended chain of direct and indirect effects within a specified time frame. Cyclical causality, in contrast, has no clear beginning or end. Instead, it is characterized by simultaneous or sequential feedback loops. Because it is cyclical it is often associated with "the chicken-and-egg" problem, that is, the difficulty of ascertaining what comes first. Yet another approach is reciprocal causality, according to which the action by one person generates its own independent response by another. Whether simultaneous or sequential, reciprocal causality implies a process whereby actors impact each other.

The problem with linear causality in policy and research is the premise that what matters can be "carved out" of reality and insulated from other factors than those posted in the framework. The notion of linearity makes analysis look easy, but it becomes especially questionable when applied to the field of politics. The latter is interactive and transactional. Action, therefore, creates counteraction. This study has shown that African government leaders respond to pressures to democratize by creating their own governance niches that make sense in their national or local context. Their response may be positive or negative, but it involves creativity, not just a compliance with pressures to democratize. It has also shown that civil society is not merely adhering to government laws and regulations but takes initiatives to promote its own agenda. Politics is more dialectic than deterministic. In the African cases, it is not as much a conflict between capital and labour since the principal social cleavages are not anchored in the economic production process but in the rivalry between communities of consumption that wish to secure as large a share as possible of government resources.

## 9.6   A REALIST THEORY

Realism is usually associated with the study of International Relations and refers to the variable presence of interest and power in the international arena and thus a form of politics that is characterized by competition rather than co-operation, compromise rather than co-ordination. International Relations scholars have provided several versions of what realism is all about and they disagree about how much guidance it offers for explanatory purposes. What they do agree upon is that unlike the idealists in the liberal tradition, they emphasize the role that interest, honour, or fear play in determining relations among states. As this study has shown, these factors are at play also in national politics in countries where the political system is not an already institutionalized hierarchy but instead is in the process of being stabilized. As it is in the study of international politics, realism serves as a counterweight to the more optimistic assumptions inherent in liberal theory. Its relevance and significance have grown in recent years as more and more countries display forms of politics in which self-interest, honour, and fear are prominent. Democratic backsliding and the growth of authoritarianism are the scholarly terms that confirm this phenomenon. Realism, however, is not necessarily associated with doomsday scenarios. It is true that identity politics enhances the risk that both honour and fear may influence politics and increase the probability of civil conflict. Most countries, however, have institutional mechanisms for managing the conditions that tend to produce such conflicts. This book has shown that the majority of African governments are successful in doing so. Realism in Comparative Politics, therefore, is an appropriate mid-level theory to capture the forms of politics that have been side-lined by the positivist inclinations of democratic theory. It has a growing role to play in Comparative Politics theorizing as new research interests are emerging in the field.

## 9.7 CONCLUSIONS

This book has highlighted the issues associated with using a general theory with claims to universal validity. This mode of theorizing stirs up three controversies that limit its robustness. The *first* is its partiality. By choosing the historical legacy of one region or a few select cases as the foundation, theory speaks to some countries but not others. This is evident in the literature on democratization in which to be "developing" or "democratizing" is not problematized. By merely focusing on the degree of democracy in countries around the world, it leaves out the real issues associated with modernization and constitutional reform. This book has argued that more attention needs to be paid to the structural conditions that shape the variations in level of democratic development. The *second* controversy relates to its determinism. This is an issue that dates all the way back to the early days of the field when theorists identified social change in terms of degree of structural differentiation in society. This way of thinking about politics has reappeared in the application of democratic theory. Democratization is presented as a virtual inevitability. Research centres on how well countries proceed in that direction – or fall behind by becoming increasingly autocratic. Politics is generally more open-ended with no pre-set endpoint. The *third* controversy is the inclination to produce scales that do not take into consideration where countries come from in their effort to democratize. There is no fairness in the comparative scores that dominate measurements of democracy. Setting developed and developing countries side by side is like comparing apples and oranges. It is only by taking into consideration the structural constraints and opportunities in each country – or region – that cross-country comparison becomes convincing. This approach is more cumbersome and labour-intensive than merely relying on numbers aggregated from surveys, whether based on expert evaluations or public opinion. Yet, that is the way to go.

I leave the reader with an upbeat note: there is no shortage of challenges for researchers who wish to bring theorizing in our field to the next station. The state of the field in the 2020s may not be quite as spirited as it was in the 1960s, but with the fading away of democratic theory as a principal guide to analysis, the field is entering a "post-democratic" period with similar challenges to rethink theory.

# References

Acemoglu, Daron and James A. Robinson 2012. *Why Nations Fail: The Origins of Power, Prosperity and Poverty*. New York: Crown Publishers.

Adebanwi, Wole and Ebenezer Obadare (eds.) 2015. *Democracy and Prebendalism in Nigeria: Critical Perspectives*. New York: Palgrave Macmillan.

Adejumobi, Said 2015. *Democratic Renewal in Africa: Trends and Discourses*. Berlin: Springer Verlag.

Ajayi, Ade J. F. and Michael Crowder 1976. *History of West Africa*, volume 1. London: Longman.

Ake, Claude 1996. *Democracy and Development in Africa*. Washington, DC: Brookings Institution Press.

Alden, Christopher 2013. "China and the Long March into African Agriculture", *Cahiers Agricultures*, vol. 22, no 1, pp. 16–21.

Almond, Gabriel A. 1960. "A Theoretical Framework for Functional Analysis", in G. A. Almond and J. S. Coleman (eds.), *The Politics of the Developing Areas*, pp. 1–64. Princeton, NJ: Princeton University Press.

Almond, Gabriel A. and James S. Coleman (eds.) 1960. *The Politics of the Developing Areas*. Princeton, NJ: Princeton University Press.

Almond, Gabriel A. and Sidney Verba 1963. *The Civic Culture: Political Attitudes and Democracy in Five Nations*. Princeton, NJ: Princeton University Press.

Amin, Samir 1976. *Unequal Development: An Essay on the Social Formations of Peripheral Capitalism*. New York: Monthly Review Press.

Andrews, Matt 2013. *The Limits of Institutional Reform in Development: Changing Rules for Realistic Solutions*. Cambridge: Cambridge University Press.

Andrews, Matt, Lant Pritchard, and Michael Woolcock 2012. "Escaping Capability Traps through Problem-Driven Iterative Adaptation (PDIA)", *Working Paper No. 299*, Center for Global Development, Harvard University.

Anyang Nyong'o, Peter (ed.) 1987. *Popular Struggles for Democracy in Africa*. London: Zed Books.

Arreola, Leonard 2013. "Protesting and Policing in Multi-Ethnic Authoritarian States", *Comparative Politics*, vol. 45, no. 2, pp. 147–68.

Arrighi, Giovanni and John J. Saul (eds.) 1973. *Essays on the Political Economy of Africa*. New York: Monthly Review Press.

Atieno-Odhiambo, Eisha S. 2002. "Hegemonic Enterprises and Instrumentalities of Survival: Ethnicity and Democracy in Kenya", *African Studies*, vol. 61, no. 2, pp. 223–49.

Bakken, Ingrid Vik and Siri Aas Rustad 2018. "Conflict Trends in Africa, 1989–2017", *Conflict Trends No. 6*. Oslo: International Peace Research Institute in Oslo (PRIO).

Bartolini, Stefano and Peter Mair 1990. *Identity, Competition, and Electoral Availability: The Stabilisation of European Electorates 1885–1985*. Oxford: Oxford University Press.

Bates, Robert H. 1981. *Markets and States in Tropical Africa: The Political Basis of Agricultural Policies*. Berkeley: University of California Press.

Bayart, Jean-François 1993. *The State in Africa: The Politics of the Belly*. London: Longman.

Beetham, David 1994. *Defining and Measuring Democracy*. Thousand Oaks, CA: SAGE.

Benhabib, Seyla 1996. *Democracy and Difference: Testing the Boundaries of the Political*. Princeton, NJ: Princeton University Press.

Berk, Gerald and Dennis Galvan 2009. "How People Experience and Change Institutions: A Field Guide to Creative Syncretism", *Theory and Society*, vol. 38, no. 6, pp. 543–80.

Berman, Bruce 1998. "Ethnicity, Patronage, and the African State: The Politics of Uncivil Nationalism", *African Affairs*, vol. 98, no. 388, pp. 305–41.

Bermeo, Nancy 2016. "On Democratic Backsliding", *Journal of Democracy*, vol. 27, no. 1, pp. 5–19.

Berry, Sara S. 1993. *No Condition Is Permanent: The Social Dynamics of Agrarian Change in Sub-Saharan Africa*. Madison, WI: University of Wisconsin Press.

Bessette, Joseph M. 1994. *The Mild Voice of Reason: Deliberative Democracy and American National Government*. Chicago: University of Chicago Press.

Blanshe, Musinguzi 2012. "Uganda: Why Is the Middle Class Shrinking Despite Its Economic Growth?" *The Africa Report*, London, 27 September.

Bleck, Jaimie and Nicolas van de Walle 2012. "Valence Issues in African Elections: Navigating Uncertainty and the Weight of the Past", *Comparative Political Studies*, vol. 46, no. 11, pp. 1394–421.

Blommaert, Jan 2013. "State Ideology and Language in Tanzania", *Tilbury Papers in Culture Studies No 80*. Tilburg, The Netherlands: Tilburg University.

Bogaards, Matthijs 2009. "How to Classify Hybrid Regimes? Defective Democracy and Electoral Authoritarianism", *Democratization*, vol. 16, no. 2, pp. 399–423.

Bohman, James F. 1998. "The Coming of Age of Deliberative Democracy", *Journal of Political Philosophy*, vol. 6, no. 4, pp. 399–423.

Boone, Catherine 2014. *Property and Political Order in Africa. Land Rights and the Structure of Politics*. New York: Cambridge University Press.

Booth, David 2011. "Aid, Institutions and Governance: What Have We Learned?", *Development Policy Review*, vol. 29, Special Issue, pp. s1–s21.

Booth, David 2015. "Still Watering White Elephants? The Blueprint versus Process Debate Thirty Years On", in A. Mette Kjaer, Lars Engberg-Pedersen and Lars Buur (eds.), *Perspectives on Politics, Production and Public Administration in Africa: Essays in Honour of Ole Therkildsen*, pp. 11–26. Copenhagen: Danish Institute of International Studies.

Booth, David and Frederick Golooba-Mutebi 2012. "Developmental Patrimonialism? The Case of Rwanda", *African Affairs*, vol. 111, no. 444, pp. 379–403.

Boserup, Ester 1965. *The Conditions of Agricultural Growth: the Economics of Agrarian Change under Population Pressure*. London: Allen & Unwin.

Botchwey, Kwesi 1981. *Transforming the "Periphery": A Study of the Struggle of the Social Forces in Ghana for Democracy and National Sovereignty*. New York: The United Nations.

Bratton, Michael 2010. "The Meanings of Democracy: Anchoring the D-Word in Africa", *Journal of Democracy*, vol. 21, no. 4, pp. 106–13.

Bratton, Michael and Nicolas van de Walle 1997. *Democratic Experiments in Africa: Regime Transition in Comparative Perspective*. New York: Cambridge University Press.

Bratton, Michael and Richard Houessou 2014. "Demand for Democracy Is Rising in Africa, but Most Political Leaders Fail to Deliver", *Afrobarometer Policy Paper No. 11*. Johannesburg: IDASA.

Braybrooke, David and Charles E. Lindblom 1963. *A Strategy for Decision: Policy Evaluation as a Social Process*. New York: The Free Press.

Brockway, Fenner 1963. *African Socialism*. London: Bodley Head.

Calhoun, Craig (ed.) 1992. *Habermas and the Public Sphere*. Cambridge, MA: MIT Press.

Caporaso, James A. 2000. "Comparative Politics: Coherence and Diversity", *Comparative Political Studies*, vol. 33, no. 6–7, pp. 699–702.

Carboni, Andrea and Clionadh Raleigh 2021. "Regime Cycles and Political Change in African Autocracies", *The Journal of Modern African Studies*, vol. 59, no. 4, pp. 415–37.

Carneiro, Goncalo et al. 2015. "Support to Capacity Development – Identifying Good Practice in Swedish Development Cooperation", *Evaluation Report 2015:2*. Stockholm: Sida.

Carothers, Thomas and Diane De Gramont 2013. *Development Aid Confronts Politics: The Almost Revolution*. Washington, DC: Carnegie Endowment for International Peace.

Chayanov, Alexander 1966. *The Theory of Peasant Economy*. Homewood, IL: Richard Irwin.

Cheeseman, Nic 2015. *Democracy in Africa: Successes, Failures, and the Struggle for Reform*. Cambridge: Cambridge University Press.

Chege, Michael 1995. "Democracy's Future: Between Africa's Extremes". *Journal of Democracy*, vol. 6, no. 2, pp. 52–64.

Chlouba, Vladimir, Daniel S. Smith, and Seamus Wagner 2021. "Early Statehood and Support for Autocratic Rule", *Comparative Political Studies*, vol. 55, no. 4, pp. 688–724.

CIVICUS 2020. *State of Civil Society Report 2020*. Johannesburg: CIVICUS.

Clarke, Gerald et al. (eds.) 2008. *Development, Civil Society and Faith-Based Organizations*. London: Palgrave Macmillan.

Cliffe, Lionel (ed.) 1967. *One Party Democracy: The 1965 Tanzania General Elections*. Nairobi: East African Publishing House.

Cohen, Joshua and Charles Sabel 1997. "Direct-Deliberative Polyarchy", *European Law Journal*, vol. 3, no. 4, pp. 313–42.

Coleman, James S. and Carl G. Rosberg (eds.) 1964. *Political Parties and National Integration in Tropical Africa*. Berkeley and Los Angeles: University of California Press.

Coleman, James Smooth 1965. *Nigeria: Background to Nationalism*. Berkeley and Los Angeles: University of California Press.

Collier, Paul and Anke Hoeffler 1998. "On Economic Causes of Civil War", *Oxford Economic Papers*, vol. 50, no. 4, pp. 563–70.

Collier, Ruth Berins and David Collier 1978. *Shaping the Political Arena: Critical Junctures, the Labour Movement and Regime Dynamics in Latin America*. Notre Dame, IN: University of Notre Dame Press.

Connah, Graham 1987. *African Civilizations: Precolonial States and Cities in Tropical Africa: An Archaeological Perspective*. Cambridge: Cambridge University Press.

Cooper, Frederick 1996. *Decolonization and African Society: The Labour Question in French and British Africa*. Cambridge: Cambridge University Press.

Coppedge, Michael 1994. *Strong Men and Lame Ducks: Presidential Partyarchy and Factionalism in Venezuela*. Stanford, CA: Stanford University Press.

Coppedge, Michael 2012. *Democratization and Research Methods*. New York: Cambridge University Press.

Coquery-Vidrovitch, Catherine 1978. "Research on an African Mode of Production", in D. Seddon (ed.), *Relations of Production: Marxist Approaches to Economic Anthropology*, pp. 261–88. London: Frank Cass.

Coquery-Vidrovitch, Catherine 1988. *Africa: Endurance and Change South of the Sahara*, translated by D. Maisel. Berkeley: University of California Press.

Coulson, Andrew 1982. *Tanzania: A Political Economy*. Oxford: Clarendon Press.

Crisafulli, Patricia and Andrea Redmond 2014. *Rwanda Inc.: How a Devastated Nation Became an Economic Model for the Developing World*. London: St. Martin's Griffin.

Crowder, Michael and Obaro Ikime (eds.) 1970. *West African Chiefs. Their Changing Status under Colonial Rule and Independence*. Ile-Ife: University of Ife Press.

Dahl, Robert 1971. *On Democracy*. New Haven, CT: Yale University Press.

Dalton, Russell J. and Martin P. Wattenberg 2003. *Parties without Partisans: Political Change in Advanced Industrial Democracies*. Oxford: Oxford University Press.

Diamond, Larry, Juan Linz, and Seymour M. Lipset (eds.) 1988. *Democracy in Developing Countries: Africa*. Boulder, CO: Lynne Rienner.

Diop, Cheikh Anta 1976. *Precolonial Black Africa*. Newport, CT: Lawrence Hill & Company.

Doorenspleet, Renske and Lia Nijzink (eds.) 2013. *One-Party Dominance in African Democracies*. Boulder, CO: Lynne Rienner.

Downs, Anthony 1957. *An Economic Theory of Democracy*. New York: Harper.

Dryzek, John 2010. *Foundations and Frontiers of Deliberative Democracy*. Oxford: Oxford University Press.

Dunleavy, Patrick and Francoise Boucek 2003. "Constructing the Number of Parties", *Party Politics*, vol. 9, no. 3, pp. 291–315.

Durkheim, Emile 1953. *Sociology and Philosophy*, translated by D. F. Pocock. Toronto: The Free Press.

Durotoye, Adeolu 2017. "Democracy and Political Development", in Samuel Ojo Oloruntoba and Toyin Falola (eds.), *The Palgrave Handbook of Africa Politics, Governance and Development*, pp. 471–83. London: Palgrave Macmillan.

Duverger, Maurice 1954. *Political Parties and Their Activities in the Modern State*. New York: Wiley.

Dwyer, Maggie and Thomas Molony 2019. *Social Media and Politics in Africa: Democracy, Censorship and Security*. London: Zed Books.

Easterly, William and Ross Levine 1997. "Africa's Growth Tragedy: Policies and Ethnic Divisions", *The Quarterly Journal of Economics*, vol. 112, no. 4, pp. 1203–50.

Easton, David 1969. "The New Revolution in Political Science", *American Political Science Review*, vol. 63, no. 4 (December), pp. 1051–61.

Ekeh, Peter 1975. "Colonialism and the Two Publics in Africa: A Theoretical Statement", *Comparative Studies in Society and History*, vol. 17, no. 1, pp. 91–112.

Elischer, Sebastian 2013. *Political Parties in Africa: Ethnicity and Party Formation*. New York: Cambridge University Press.

Ellis, Markman 2004. *The Coffee House: A Cultural History*. London: Weidenfeld & Nicolson.

Elster, Jon 1998. *Deliberative Democracy*. Cambridge: Cambridge University Press.

Englund, Harri 2006. *Prisoners of Freedom: Human Rights and the African Poor*. Berkeley: University of California Press.

Entman, Robert M. 2001. "Contestable Categories and Public Opinion", *Political Communication*, vol. 10, no. 3, pp. 231–42.

Erdmann, Gero 2004. "Party Research: Western Bias and the 'African Labyrinth'", *Democratization*, vol. 11, no. 3, pp. 63–87.

Esping-Andersen, Gösta 1985. *Politics against Markets: The Social Democratic Road to Power*. Princeton, NJ: Princeton University Press.

Evans, Peter, Dieter Rueschemeyer, and Theda Skocpol (eds.) 1985. *Bringing the State Back In*. New York: Cambridge University Press.

Fortes, Meyer and Edward E. Evans Pritchard 1940. *African Political Systems*. Oxford: Oxford University Press.

Francis, Paul and Robert James 2003. "Balancing Rural Poverty Reduction and Citizen Participation: The Contradictions of Uganda's Decentralization Program", *World Development*, vol. 31, no. 2, pp. 325–37.

Freedom House 2020. *Freedom in the World, 2020*. Washington, DC: Freedom House.

Friedland, William H. and Carl G. Rosberg 1964. *African Socialism*. Stanford, CA: Stanford University Press.

Frinjuah, John P. and Josephine Appiah-Nyamekye 2018. "Time to Redeem Africa from Corruption", *Afrobarometer Paper*, January. Johannesburg: IDASA.

Fukuyama, Francis 1992. *End of History and the Last Man*. New York: The Free Press.

Geddes, Barbara 2010. *Paradigms and Sand Castles: Theory-Building and Research Methods in Comparative Politics*. Ann Arbor, MI: University of Michigan Press.

Geshiere, Peter 2009. *The Perils of Belonging: Autochthony, Citizenship, and Exclusion in Africa and Europe*. Chicago: University of Chicago Press.

Geshiere, Peter and Francis Nyamnjoh 2000. "Capitalism and Autochthony: The Seesaw of Mobility and Belonging", *Public Culture*, vol. 12, no. 2, pp. 423–52

Giblin, James C. 1995. *When Plague Strikes: The Black Death, Smallpox, Aids.* New York: Harper Collins.

Gibson, Clark C and Barak D. Hoffman 2013. "Coalitions, not Conflicts: Ethnicity, Political Institutions, and Expenditure in Africa", *Comparative Politics*, vol. 45, no. 3, pp. 273–90.

Gilljam, Mikael and Henrik Oscarsson 1996. "Mapping the Nordic Political Space", *Scandinavian Political Studies*, vol. 9, no. 1, pp. 25–44.

Goody, Jack 1971. *Technology, Tradition, and the State in Africa.* Oxford: Oxford University Press.

Goody, Jack 1976. *Production and Reproduction: A Comparative Study of the Domestic Domain.* Cambridge: Cambridge University Press.

Gordon, Colin 1991. "Governmentality", in G. Burchell, C. Gordon, and P. Miller (eds.), *The Foucault Effect: Studies in Governmentality*, pp. 87–104. Chicago: University of Chicago Press.

Gramsci, Antonio 2011. *Letters from Prison*, vol. 1–3, edited by Frank Rosengarten. New York: Columbia University Press.

Green, Elliott 2011. "Patronage as Institutional Choice: Evidence from Rwanda and Uganda", *Comparative Politics*, vol. 43, no. 4, pp. 421–38.

Grundy W. Kenneth 1996. "African Explanations of Underdevelopment: The Theoretical Basis for Political Action", *The Review of Politics*, vol. 28, no. 1, pp. 64–65.

Gutkind, Peter 1970. *The Passing of Tribal Man in Africa.* Leiden: E. J. Brill.

Gutkind, Peter and Immanuel Wallerstein (eds.) 1976. *The Political Economy of Contemporary Africa.* London: SAGE.

Gutmann, Amy and Dennis Thompson 2002. "Deliberative Democracy beyond Process", *Journal of Political Philosophy*, vol. 10, no. 2, pp. 153–74.

Gwen, Elliott 2011. "Patronage as Institutional Choice: Evidence from Rwanda and Uganda", *Comparative Politics*, vol. 43, no. 4, pp.421–38.

Habermas, Jürgen 1981. *The Theory of Communicative Action*, vol. 1–2. Cambridge: Cambridge University Press.

Haggard, Stephan and Robert R. Kaufman 2016. *Dictators and Democrats: Masses, Elites and Regime Change.* Princeton, NJ: Princeton University Press.

Hansen, Holger B. and Michael Twaddle (eds.) 1998. *Uganda Now: Between Decay and Development.* Oxford: James Currey.

Harris, Adam S. and Erin Hearn 2018. "Taking to the Streets: Protest as an Expression of Political Preferences in Africa", *Comparative Political Studies*, vol. 52, no 8, pp. 1169–99.

Hart, Keith 1982. *The Political Economy of West African Agriculture*. Cambridge: Cambridge University Press.

Hasselskog, Malin and Isabell Schierenbeck 2015. "National Policy in Local Practice: The Case of Rwanda", *Third World Quarterly*, vol. 36, no. 5, pp. 350–66.

Hay, Colin 2002. *Political Analysis: A Critical Introduction*. Basingstoke: Palgrave.

Hearn, Julie 2000. "Aiding Democracy? Donors and Civil Society in South Africa", *Third World Quarterly*, vol. 21, no. 5, pp. 815–30.

Helmke, Gretchen and Steven Levitsky 2006. "Informal Institutions and Comparative Politics: A Research Agenda". *Perspectives on Politics*, vol. 2, no. 4, pp. 725–40.

Herbst, Jeffrey 2000. *States and Power in Africa: Comparative Lessons in Authority and Control*. Princeton, NJ: Princeton University Press.

Herbst, Jeffrey 2014. *States and Power in Africa: Comparative Lessons in Authority and Control*, second edition. Princeton, NJ: Princeton University Press.

Himmelstrand, Ulf, Kabiru Kinyanjui, and Edward K. Mburugu (eds.) 1994. *African Perspectives on Development: Controversies, Dilemmas and Debates*. London: James Currey.

Hodge, Joseph Morgan 2007. *Triumph of the Expert: Agrarian Doctrines of Development and the Legacies of British Colonialism*. Miami, OH: Ohio University Press.

Huber, Evelyne and John D. Stephens 2001. *Development and Crisis of the Welfare State: Parties and Policies in Global Markets*. Chicago: University of Chicago Press.

Huggins, Chris 2017. *Agricultural Reform in Rwanda: Authoritarianism, Markets and Zones of Governance*. London: Zed Books.

Hui, Victoria Tin-bor 2005. *War and State Formation in Ancient China and Early Modern Europe*. Cambridge: Cambridge University Press.

Huntington, Samuel P. 1965. "Political Development and Political Decay", *World Politics*, vol. 17, no. 3, pp. 386–430.

Huntington, Samuel P. 1968. *Political Order in Changing Society*. New Haven, CT: Yale University Press.

Huntington, Samuel P. 1984. "Will More Countries Become Democratic?", *Political Science Quarterly*, vol. 99, no. 2, pp. 193–218.

Huntington, Samuel P. 1991. *The Third Wave of Democratization*. Norman, OK: Oklahoma University Press.

Hyden, Goran 1969. *Political Development in Rural Tanzania*. Nairobi: East African Publishing House.

Hyden, Goran 1980. *Beyond Ujamaa in Tanzania: Underdevelopment and an Uncaptured Peasantry*. Berkeley: University of California Press.

Hyden, Goran 1980. *Beyond Ujamaa in Tanzania: Underdevelopment and an Uncaptured Peasantry*. London: Heinemann.

Hyden, Göran and Marina Buch Kristensen 2019. "Democracy in African Governance: Seeing and Doing It Differently", *EBA Report 2019:09*. Stockholm: Expert Group for Aid Analysis (EBA).

Hyden, Goran, Kazihuko Sugimura, and Tadasu Tsuruta (eds.) 2020. *Rethinking African Agriculture: How Non-Agrarian Factors Shape Rural Livelihoods*. Basingstoke: Routledge.

Ibhawoh, Bonny and Jeremiah I. Dibua 2003. "Deconstructing Ujamaa: The Legacy of Julius Nyerere in the Quest for Social and Economic Development in Africa", *African Journal of Political Science*, vol. 8, no. 1, pp. 59–83.

Iliffe, John 1995. *The Africans: A History of the Continent*. Cambridge: Cambridge University Press.

Inglehart, Ronald and Pippa Norris 2003. *Rising Tide: Gender Equality and Cultural Change around the World*. Cambridge: Cambridge University Press.

Jackson, Robert H. and Carl G. Rosberg 1982. *Personal Rule in Black Africa: Prince, Autocrat, Prophet, Tyrant*. Berkeley: University of California Press.

Johnson, Chalmers 1982. *MITI and the Japanese Miracle: The Growth of Industrial Policy, 1925–75*. Stanford, CA: Stanford University Press.

Joseph, Richard 1987. *Democracy and Prebendal Politics in Nigeria: The Rise and Fall of the Second Republic*. Cambridge: Cambridge University Press.

Joseph, Richard 1999. *State, Conflict and Democracy in Africa*. Boulder, CO: Lynne Rienner.

Kabeer, Naila 1994. *Reversed Realities: Gender Hierarchies in Development Thought*. London: Verso.

Kakeya, Makoto 1976. "Subsistence Ecology of the Tongwe, Tanzania", *Kyoto University African Studies*, vol. 10, pp. 143–212.

Kakeya, Makoto 1986. "Livelihood Structure of Traditional Peasants: A Case of the Tongwe", in Juni'chiro Itani and Jiro Tanaka (eds.), *Anthropology of Natural Society*, pp. 218–42. Kyoto: Academia Publisher.

Kakeya, Makoto 2018. *Collected Works of Makoto Kakeya, volume III*. Kyoto: Kyoto University Press.

Karatani, Kojin 2014. *The Structure of World History: From Modes of Production to Modes of Exchange*. Durham, NC and London: Duke University Press.

Katzenstein, Peter 1985. *Small States in World Markets: Industrial Policy in Europe*. Ithaca, NY: Cornell University Press.

Keman, Hans 2014. "Democratic Performance of Parties and Legitimacy in Europe", *West European Politics*, vol. 37, no. 2, pp. 309–330.

Kiiza, Julius, Sabiti Makara, and Lise Rakner (eds.) 2008. *Electoral Democracy in Uganda*. Kampala: Fountain Publishers.

Kitschelt, Herbert 1999. *Post-Communist Party Systems*. New York: Cambridge University Press.

Kopytoff, Igor 1989. *The African Frontier: The Reproduction of Traditional African Societies*. Bloomington, IN: Indiana University Press.

Kramon, Eric and Daniel Posner 2013. *Who Benefits from Distributive Politics: How the Outcome One Studies Affects the Answer One Gets*. New York: Cambridge University Press.

Kriesi, Hanspeter 1998. "The Transformation of Cleavage Politics – The 1997 Stein Rokkan Lecture", *European Journal of Political Research*, vol. 33, no. 2, pp. 165–85.

Krönke, Mattias, Sara J. Lockwood, and Robert Mattes 2020. "Party Footprints in Africa: Measuring Local Party Presence across the Region", *Afrobarometer Working Paper No. 185*. Accra: Centre for Democratic Development.

Kuenzi, Michelle and Gina Lambright 2001. "Party System Institutionalization in 30 African Countries", *Party Politics*, vol. 7, no. 4, pp. 437–68.

Kuhn, Thomas 1962. *The Structure of Scientific Revolutions*. Chicago: University of Chicago Press.

Kuper, Adam 1988. *The Invention of Primitive Society: Transformations of an Illusion*. London: Routledge.

Laakso, Marku and Rein Taagepera 1979. "'Effective' Number of Parties: A Measure with Application to West Europe", *Comparative Political Studies*, vol. 12, no. 1, pp. 3–27.

LeBas, Adrienne 2011. *From Protest to Party: Party-Building and Democratization in Africa*. Oxford: Oxford University Press.

Lehmbruch, Gerhard and Philippe C. Schmitter (eds.) 1982. *Patterns of Corporatist Policy-Making*. London and Beverly Hills: SAGE.

Lemarchand, René 1970. *Ruanda and Burundi*. New York: Praeger.

Lemarchand, René (ed.) 1977. *African Kingships in Perspective*. London: Frank Cass.

Levi, Margaret 1989. *Of Rule and Revenue*. Berkeley: University of California Press.

Levitsky, Steven and Daniel Ziblatt 2018. *How Democracies Die*. New York: Random House.

Levitsky, Steven and Lucan Way 2010. *Competitive Authoritarianism: Hybrid Regimes after the Cold War*. New York: Cambridge University Press.

Levy, Brian 2014. *Working with the Grain: Integrating Governance with Growth in Development Strategies*. New York: Oxford University Press.

Levy, Brian and Michael Walton 2013. "Institutions, Incentives and Service Provision: Bringing Politics Back In", *ESID Working Paper No 8*. Effective States and Inclusive Development Research Centre, University of Manchester.

Leys, Colin 1975. *Underdevelopment in Kenya: The Political Economy of Neo-Colonialism*. London: Heinemann.

Lieberman, Victor B. 2003. *Strange Parallels: Southeast Asia in Global Context, c. 800–1830*. Cambridge: Cambridge University Press.

Lijphart, Arend 1977. *Democracy in Plural Societies: A Comparative Exploration*. New Haven, CT: Yale University Press.

Lijphart, Arend 1984. *Democracies: Patterns of Majoritarian and Consensus Government in Twenty-One Countries*. New Haven, CT: Yale University Press.

Lindberg, Staffan 2003. "It Is Our Time to 'Chop': Do Elections in Africa Feed Neo-Patrimonialism Rather Than Counteract It?" *Democratization*, vol. 10, no. 2, pp. 121–40.

Lindblom, Charles E. 1959. "The Science of 'Muddling Through'". *Public Administration Review*, vol. 19, no. 1, pp. 79–88.

Lipset, Seymour M. and Stein Rokkan (eds.) 1967. *Party Systems and Voter Alignments: Cross-National Perspectives*. New York: The Free Press.

Lipset, Seymour Martin 1959. "Some Social Requisites of Democracy: Economic Development and Political Legitimacy", *American Political Science Review*, vol. 53, no. 1, pp. 69–105.

Lipset, Seymour Martin 1960. *Political Man: The Social Bases of Politics*. New York: Doubleday.

Long, James D., Karuti Kanyinga, Karen E. Ferree, and Clark Gibson 2013. "Choosing Peace Over Democracy", *Journal of Democracy*, vol. 24, no. 3, pp. 140–55.

Lopez, Ricardo A. and Barbara Weinstein 2012. *The Making of the Middle Class: Toward a Transnational History*. Durham, NC: Duke University Press.

Low, Linda 2004. *Developmental States: Relevancy, Redundancy or Reconfiguration*. Hauppauge, NY: Nova Science Publishers.

Lührmann, Anna and Staffan I. Lindberg 2019. "A Third Wave of Autocratization Is Here: What Is New About It?", *Democratization*, vol. 26, no. 7, pp. 1095–1113.

Lynch, Gabrielle and Peter VonDoepp (eds.) 2020. *Routledge Handbook on Democratization in Africa*. New York: Routledge.

MacLean, Lauren 2010. *Informal Institutions and Citizenship in Rural Africa: Risk and Reciprocity in Ghana and the Ivory Coast*. New York: Cambridge University Press.

Maddox, Gregory H., James L. Giblin, and Isaria N. Kimambo (eds.) 1996. *Custodians of the Land: Ecology and Nature in the History of Tanzania*. Athens, OH: Ohio University Press.

Mainwaring, Scott (ed.) 2018. *Party Systems in Latin America: Institutionalization, Decay and Collapse*. New York: Cambridge University Press.

Mainwaring, Scott and Frances Hagopian 2005. *The Third Wave of Democratization in Latin America: Advances and Setbacks*. Cambridge: Cambridge University Press.

Mainwaring, Scott and Edurne Zoco 2007. "Political Sequences and the Stabilization of Interparty Competition: Electoral Volatility in Old and New Democracies", *Party Politics*, vol. 13, no. 2, pp. 155–78.

Mainwaring, Scott and Timothy R. Scully (eds.) 1995. *Building Democratic Institutions: Party Systems in Latin America*. Stanford, CA: Stanford University Press.

Mair, Peter 1997. *Party System Change: Approaches and Interpretations*. Oxford: Oxford University Press.

Mamdani, Mahmood 1996. *Citizen and Subject: Contemporary Africa and the Legacy of Late Colonialism*. Princeton, NJ: Princeton University Press.

Mamdani, Mahmood 2001. *When Victims Become Killers: Colonialism, Nativism and the Genocide in Rwanda*. Princeton NJ: Princeton University Press.

Manji, Firoze and Carl O'Coill 2002. "The Missionary Position: NGOs and Development in Africa", *International Affairs*, vol. 78, no. 3, pp. 567–84.

Mansbridge, Jane 1999. "Everyday Talk in the Deliberative System", in S. Macedo (ed.), *Deliberative Politics: Essays on Democracy and Disagreement*, pp. 211–42, Oxford: Oxford University Press.

Maquet, Jacques J. 1961. *The Premise of Inequality in Ruanda*. London: Routledge (Republished by Routledge 2020).

Markovitz, Irving Leonard 1969. *Leopold Senghor and the Politics of Negritude*. New York: Atheneum Publishers.

Mbembe, Achille 2001. *On the Postcolony*. Berkeley: University of California Press.

Mbembe, Achille 2021. *Out of the Dark Night: Essays on Decolonization*. New York: Columbia University Press.

McCann, James 1995. *People of the Plow: An Agricultural History of Ethiopia, 1800–1950*. Madison, WI: University of Wisconsin Press.

McCombs, Maxwell 2004. *Setting the Agenda: The Mass Media and Public Opinion*. Cambridge: Polity Press.

Mercer, Claire 2002. "NGOs, Civil Society and Democratization: A Critical Review of the Literature", *Progress in Development Studies*, vol. 2, no. 1, pp. 5–22.

Meyerrose, Anna M. 2020. "The Unintended Consequences of Democracy Promotion: International Organizations and Democratic Backsliding", *Comparative Political Studies*, vol. 53, nos. 10–11, pp. 1547–81.

Migdal, Joel 1988. *Strong Societies and Weak States: State-Society Relations and State Capabilities in the Third World*. New Haven, CT: Yale University Press.

Mkandawire, Thandika and Adebayo Olukoshi 1995. *Between Liberation and Oppression: The Politics of Structural Adjustment in Africa*. Dakar: CODESRIA Press.

Moe, Terry 2005. "Power and Political Institutions", *Perspectives on Politics*, vol. 3, no. 2, pp. 215–33.

Moller, Jorgen and Svend Erik Skaaning 2018. *Requisites of Democracy: Conceptualisation, Measurement and Explanation*. Abingdon: Routledge.

Moore, Barrington Jr 1966. *Social Origins of Dictatorship and Democracy: Lord and Peasant in the Making of the Modern World*. Princeton, NJ: Princeton University Press.

Moy, Patricia and Dietram E. Scheufele 2000. "Media Effects on Political and Social Trust", *Journalism and Mass Communication Quarterly*, vol. 77, no. 4, pp. 744–59.

Mozzafar, Shaheen and James R. Scarritt 2005. "The Puzzle of African Party Systems", *Party Politics*, vol. 11, no. 4, pp. 399–421.

Mudde, Cas and Cristobal Rovira Kaltwasser 2012. *Populism in Europe and the Americas: Threat or Corrective for Democracy?* New York: Cambridge University Press.

Mudhai, Okoth F., Wisdom Tettey, and Fackson Banda (eds.) 2009. *African Media and the Digital Public Sphere*. Basingstoke: Palgrave Macmillan.

Mueller, Lisa 2018. *Political Protests in Contemporary Africa*. New York: Cambridge University Press.

Mwansasu, Bismarck U. and Cranford Pratt 1979. *Towards Socialism in Tanzania*. Toronto: University of Toronto Press.

Nakao, Sasuke 1966. *The Origin of Domesticated Plants and Agriculture*. Tokyo: Iwanami Shoten.

Ndegwa, Steven 1997. "Citizenship and Ethnicity: Examination of Two Transition Moments in Kenyan Politics", *American Political Science Review*, vol. 91, no. 3, pp. 599–616.

Newbury, Catherine 1988. *The Cohesion of Oppression: Clientship and Ethnicity in Rwanda, 1860–1960*. New York: Columbia University Press.

Niane, Djibril Tamsir (ed.) 1984. *General History of Africa, IV: Africa from the Twelfth to the Sixteenth Century*. London and Berkeley: Heinemann Educational Books and University of California Press.

Norris, Pippa 2000. *A Virtuous Circle: Political Communications in Postindustrial Societies*. Cambridge: Cambridge University Press.

Norris, Pippa and Ronald Inglehart 2019. *Cultural Backlash: Trump, Brexit, and Authoritarian Populism*. New York: Cambridge University Press.

North, Douglass C. 1990. *Institutions, Institutional Change and Economic Performance*. New York: Cambridge University Press.

North, Douglass C. 1991. "Institutions", *Journal of Economic Perspectives*, vol. 5, no. 1, pp. 97–112.

North, Douglass C., John J. Wallis, and Barry R. Weingast 2009. *Violence and Social Orders: A Framework for Interpreting Recorded Human History*. New York: Cambridge University Press.

North, Douglass C., John J. Wallis, Stephen B. Webb, and Barry R. Weingast (eds.) 2012. *In the Shadow of Violence: Politics, Economics and Problems of Development*. New York: Cambridge University Press.

Nursey-Bray, Paul F. 1980. "Tanzania: The Development Debate", *African Affairs*, vol. 9, no 314, pp. 55–78.

Nussbaum, Martha 1999. "Women and Equality: The Capabilities Approach", *International Labour Review*, vol. 138, no. 3, pp. 227–45.

Nwaubani, Ebere 2000. "Kenneth Onwuka Dike, 'Trade and Politics', and the Restoration of the African in History", *History in Africa*, vol. 27, pp. 229–48.

Obadare, Adebanwi and Larry Ebenezer (eds.) 2013. *Democracy and Prebendalism in Nigeria: Critical Interpretations*. Basingstoke: Palgrave Macmillan.

O'Donnell, Guillermo and Philippe Schmitter 1986. *Transitions from Authoritarian Rule: Tentative Conclusions about Uncertain Democracies*. Baltimore, MD: Johns Hopkins University Press.

Olan'g, Lulu and James Msami 2018. "In Tanzania, Anti-corruption Efforts Are Seen as Paying Dividends, Need Citizen Engagement", *Afrobarometer Publication AD 178*.

Osei, Anja 2018. "Elite Theory and Political Transitions: Networks of Power in Ghana and Togo", *Comparative Politics*, vol. 21, no. 1, pp. 21–42.

Ostrom, Elinor C. 1990. *Governing the Commons: The Evolution of Institutions for Collective Action*. New York: Cambridge University Press.

Portes, Jonathan, Simon Burgess, and Jake Anders 2020. "The Long-Term Outcomes of Refugees: Tracking the Progress of the East African Asians", *Journal of Refugee Studies*, vol. 34, no. 2, pp. 1967–98.

Posner, Daniel E. 2005. *Institutions and Ethnic Politics in Africa.* New York: Cambridge University Press.

Prempeh, Kwasi 2007. "Africa's 'Constitutionalism Revival': False Start or New Dawn?" *International Journal of Constitutional Law*, vol. 5, no. 3, pp. 469–506.

Prunier, Gerard 1995. *The Rwanda Crisis: The History of a Genocide.* New York: Columbia University Press.

Przeworski, Adam Michael E. Alvarez, Jose Antonio Cheibub, and Fernando Limongi 2000. *Democracy and Development; Political Institutions and Well-Being in the World, 1950–1990.* New York: Cambridge University Press.

Pye, Lucian 1967. *Aspects of Political Development.* Boston, MA: Little Brown.

Pye, Lucian and Sidney Verba 1965. *Political Culture and Political Development.* Princeton, NJ: Princeton University Press.

Radcliffe Brown, Alfred 1952. *Structure and Function in Primitive Society.* Toronto: The Free Press.

Rakner, Lise 2018. "Breaking BAD: Understanding Backlash against Democracy in Africa", *CMI Insight 2018:1.* Bergen: Chr. Michelsen Institute.

Randall, Vicky 2007. "Political Parties and Democratic Developmental States", *Development Policy Review*, vol. 25, no. 5, pp. 633–52.

Randall, Vicky and Lars Svåsand 2002. "Political Parties and Democratic Consolidation in Africa", *Democratization*, vol. 9, no. 3, pp. 30–52.

Reguero, Borja G, Inigo J. Losada, and Fernando J. Mendez 2019. "A Recent Increase in Global Wave Power as a Consequence of Oceanic Warming", *Nature Communications*, vol. 10, p. 205.

Revelli, Marco 2019. *The New Populism: Democracy Stares into the Abyss.* London: Verso.

Rich, Roland 2017. *Democracy in Crisis: Why Where, and How to Respond.* Boulder, CO: Lynne Rienner.

Richards, Paul 1985. *Indigenous Agricultural Revolution: Ecology and Food Production in West Africa.* London: Hutchinson Publisher.

Riedl, Rachel Beatty 2014. *Authoritarian Origins of Democratic Party Systems in Africa.* New York: Cambridge University Press.

Rimlinger, Gaston V. 1971. *Welfare and Industrialisation in Europe, America, and Russia.* Chichester: John Wiley & Sons.

Robinson, Piers 2001. "Theorizing the Influence of Media on World Politics: Models of Media Influence of Foreign Policy", *European Journal of Communication*, vol. 6, no. 4, pp. 523–44.

Rodney, Walter 1972. *How Europe Underdeveloped Africa.* New York: Monthly Review Press.

Rose, Richard and Ian McAllister 1986. *Voters Begin to Choose: From Closed Class to Open Elections in Britain.* Beverly Hills, CA: SAGE.

Rotberg, Robert I. and Ali A. Mazrui (eds.) 1970. *Protest and Power in Black Africa*. New York: Oxford University Press.

Rothchild, Donald S. and Victor A. Olorunsola (eds.) 1983. *State versus Ethnic Claims: African Policy Dilemmas*. Boulder, CO: Westview Press.

Rudolph, Lloyd I. and Susanne H. Rudolph 1967. *The Modernity of Tradition: Political Development in India*. Chicago: University of Chicago Press.

Rueschemeyer, Dietrich, Evelyn Huber Stephens, and John D. Stephens 1992. *Capitalist Development and Democracy*. New York: Cambridge University Press.

Rweyemamu, Anthony H. and Goran Hyden (eds.) 1975. *A Decade of Public Administration in Africa*. Nairobi: East African Literature Bureau.

Salih, Mohamed (ed.) 2003. *African Political Parties: Evolution, Institutionalization, and Governance*. Las Vegas: Pluto Press.

Sartori, Giovanni 1976. *Parties and Party Systems*. Cambridge: Cambridge University Press.

Schaffer, Fred 1998. *Democracy in Translation: Understanding Politics in an Unfamiliar Culture*. Ithaca, NY: Cornell University Press.

Schattschneider, Elmer E. 1942. *Party Government*. New York: Holt, Rinehart and Winston.

Schedler, Andreas (ed.) 2006. *Electoral Authoritarianism: The Dynamics of Unfree Competition*. Boulder, CO: Lynne Rienner.

Schumpeter, Joseph 1942. *Capitalism, Socialism, and Democracy*. New York: Harper & Brothers.

Scott, James C. 1998. *Seeing Like a State: How Certain Schemes to Improve the Human Condition Have Failed*. New Haven, CT: Yale University Press.

Scott, James C. 2009. *The Art of Not Being Governed: An Anarchist History of Upland Southeast Asia*. New Haven, CT: Yale University Press.

Scott, James C. 2017. *Against the Grain: A Deep History of the Earliest States*. New Haven, CT: Yale University Press.

Sen, Amartya 1999. *Development as Freedom*. New York: Alfred Knopf.

Sheriff, Abdul 1987. *Slaves, Spices, and Ivory in Zanzibar: Integration of an East African Commercial Empire into the World Economy, 1770–1887*. Athens, OH: Ohio University Press.

Shils, Edward 1963. "On the Comparative Study of the New States", in Clifford Geertz (ed.), *Old Societies and New States*, pp. 1–26. New York: The Free Press.

Shimada, Shumei 2006. "How Can We Perceive Social Vulnerability: Rethinking from a Case Study of the Impact of Infectious Disease on Agricultural Production in Zambia", *Research Institute on Humanity and Nature Report*, pp. 41–55. Kyoto University.

Shivji, Issa 1976. *Class Struggles in Tanzania*. Nairobi: Heinemann Educational Books.

Shivji, Issa 2021. "The Dialectics of Maguphilia and Maguphobia", *CODESRIA Bulletin Online No. 13*. Dakar: CODESRIA.

Skalník, Peter 1999. "Authority versus Power: A View from Social Anthropology", in Angela Cheater (ed.), *The Anthropology of Power. Empowerment and Disempowerment in Changing Structures*, pp. 163–74. London: Routledge.

Skocpol, Theda 1979. *States and Social Revolution: A Comparative Analysis of France, Russia and China*. New York: Cambridge University Press.

Steinmo, Sven 2010. *The Evolution of Modern States: Sweden, Japan, and the United States*. Cambridge: Cambridge University Press.

Stepan, Alfred, Juan J. Linz, and Yoghendra Yadav 2011. *Crafting State-Nations: India and Other Multinational Democracies*. Baltimore, MD: Johns Hopkins University Press.

Strand, Håvard, Siri Aas Rustad, Henrik Urdal, and Håvard Mykleiv Nygård 2019. *Trends in Armed Conflict, 1946–2018*. Oslo: International Peace Research Institute.

Sugiyama, Yuko 1987. "Maintaining a Life of Subsistence in the Bemba Village of Northeastern Zambia", *African Study Monographs*, Supplementary Issue 6, pp. 15–32.

Sundberg, Molly 2019. "Donors Dealing with 'Aid Effectiveness' Inconsistencies: National Staff in Foreign Aid Agencies in Tanzania", *Journal of Eastern African Studies*, vol. 13, no. 3, pp. 445–64.

Tilly, Charles 1990. *Coercion, Capital, and European States AD 990–1990*. Cambridge: Basil Blackwell.

Tilly, Charles (ed.) 1975. *The Formation of National States in Western Europe*. Princeton, NJ: Princeton University Press.

Tipps, Dean C. 1973. "Modernization Theory and the Comparative Study of Societies: A Critical Perspective", *Comparative Studies in Society and History*, vol. 15, no. 2, pp. 199–226.

Transparency International 2020. *Corruption Perceptions Index, 2020*. Berlin: Transparency International.

Tripp, Aili Mari 2010. *Museveni's Uganda: Paradoxes of Power in a Hybrid Regime*. Boulder, CO: Lynne Rienner.

Tshimpaka, Leon Mwamba and Christopher Changwe Nshimbi 2021. "Scaffolding the State: Faith-Based Organisations and Application of Democratic Principles in the DRC and Zambia", *Religion, State and Society*, vol. 50, no. 1, pp. 76–95.

Tsuruta, Tadasu 2020. "Missing Out on the Agrarian Revolution: The African Peasantry in Historical Perspective", in G. Hyden, K. Sugimura and T. Tsuruta (eds.), *Rethinking African Agriculture: How Non-agrarian Factors Shape Peasant Livelihoods*. Northampton, MA: Routledge.

Ueyama, Shumpei 1966. "On Social Formation", in Jiro Kawakita et al. (eds.) *Man: Anthropological Studies*, pp. 73–99. Tokyo: Chuokoron-sha.

van Biezen, Ingrid and Thomas Poguntke 2014. "The Decline in Membership-Based Politics", *Party Politics*, vol. 20, no. 2, pp. 205–16.

Van Heyningen, Elisabeth 1981. "Cape Town and the Plague of 1901", in Christopher Saunders, Howard Phillips and E. van Heyningen (eds.), *Studies in the History of Cape Town*, vol. 4, pp. 66–107, University of Cape Town.

Van Horn Melton, James 2001. *The Rise of the Public in Enlightenment Europe*. Cambridge: Cambridge University Press.

von Freyhold, Michaela 1979. *Ujamaa Villages in Tanzania: Analysis of a Socialist Experiment*. London: Heinemann.

Wai, Dunstan M. 1987. "Geoethnicity and the Margins of Autonomy in the Sudan", in D. S. Rothchild and V. A. Olorunsola (eds.) *State versus Ethnic Claims: African Policy Dilemmas*, pp. 304–30. Boulder, CO: Westview Press.

Waldner, David 2017. "Parties in Transitional Democracies: Authoritarian Legacies and Post-authoritarian Challenges in the Middle East and North Africa", in Nancy Bermeo and Deborah J, Yashar (eds.), *Parties, Movements and Democracy in the Developing World*, pp. 157–89. New York: Cambridge University Press.

Waldner, David and Ellen Lust 2018. "Unwelcome Change: Coming to Terms with Democratic Backsliding", *Annual Review of Political Science*, vol. 21, no. 1, pp. 93–113.

Webb, Paul and Stephen White (eds.) 2007. *Party Politics in New Democracies*. Oxford: Oxford University Press.

Weber, Eugen 1976. *Peasants into Frenchmen: The Modernization of Rural France, 1870–1914*. Stanford, CA: Stanford University Press.

Weingast, Barry R. and Donald A. Wittman 2006. "The Reach of Political Economy", in Barry R. Weingast and Donald A. Wittman (eds.) *The Oxford Handbook of Political Economy*, pp. 3–28. Oxford: Oxford University Press.

Whitehead, Laurence (ed.) 2001. *The International Dimensions of Democratization: Europe and the Americas*. Oxford: Oxford University Press.

Wiarda, Howard 1993. *Introduction to Comparative Politics*. New York: Harcourt Colle Publishers.

Wittfogel, Karl A. 1957. *Oriental Despotism*. New Haven, CT: Yale University Press.

Woo-Cumings, Meredith (ed.) 2001 *The Developmental State*. Ithaca, NY: Cornell University Press.

World Bank 2011. "Conflict, Security and Development", *World Development Report 2011*. Washington, DC: The World Bank.

World Bank 2019. *World Development Report 2018*. Washington, DC: The World Bank.

World Bank 2019. *World Governance Indicators, 2018*. Washington, DC: The World Bank.

Wrong, Michaela 2009. *It Is Our Time to Eat: The Story of a Kenyan Whistleblower*. Nairobi: National Council of Churches Press.

Young, Crawford T. 1976. *The Politics of Cultural Pluralism*. Madison, WI: University of Wisconsin Press.

Young, Crawford T. 1994. *The African Colonial State in Comparative Perspective*. New Haven, CT: Yale University Press.

Zolberg, Aristide 1966. *Creating Political Order: The Party States of West Africa*. Chicago: Rand McNally.

# Index

Africa. *See also* sub-Saharan Africa; *specific countries; specific topics*
agricultural development in
  agrarian bias, 37–38
  agrarian revolution and, 36–38
  international community role in, 37–38
  state development influenced by, 31–32
chiefdoms, 30–31
clan societies in, 30–31
community-based organizations in, 50
Comparative Politics studies on, 5
  conceptual approaches to, 134–35
  contextual relevance of, 135–37
  cultural factors in, 15–16
  local history in, 137–38
  in monographs, 14–15
  national independence movement as factor in, 22–23
democratization in, 7–8, 70
  by sub-region, 71
Economic Community of West African States, 72
neo-Marxism in, 17
non-governmental organizations in, 53–54
political culture in, 110–14
  clientelism and, 112
  cultural pluralism and, 110
  political participation as part of, 112–13
  through public sphere, 111–14
political parties in, 94–98
  in established democracies, 95
  formation of, 96–97
  in Ghana, 88
  in Mali, 88
  Party Presence Index, 97
  pragmatic-pluralist, 96

revolutionary-centralizing, 96
  in sub-Saharan Africa, 95
pre-colonial, 27–28
regimes in, 75
  authoritarian-modernizing, 117
  clientelist-competitive, 78–80
  through democratization, 70–72, 78–82
  by governance type, 77
  liberal democracy scores by type, 79
  monopolist-movemental, 78–80, 117
  neo-patrimonial-fractured, 117
  universalism in, 82
Sahelian civilizations, 33–35
social formations in, 43–49
  diversity of, 47–49
  flexibility of, 47–49
  political economies in, 48–49
  in pre-colonial Africa, 44–45
  primitive societies and, 43–44
  self-governance as part of, 49
  tribal societies and, 43–44
state development in, 29–36
  agricultural origins in, 31–32
  failures of, 29–36
  in Inland Africa, 35–36
  lack of influence from other civilizations, 32–34
  reliance on trade in, 34–35
  in sub-Saharan Africa, 32–34
  types of, 30–31
state-nations in, 61–66
  as bifurcated states, 62–63
  *Bula Matari*, 62
  dual identities in, 64–65
  exposure to external forces in, 61–62
  governmentality in, 64
  soft power in, 61
  transactional politics, 64–65

Printed by Printforce, United Kingdom